ETHNICITY IN FOCUS
The South African Case

By Simon Bekker

ETHNICITY IN FOCUS
The South African Case

By Simon Bekker

Indicator SA
Issue Focus

December 1993

To my son
Duncan Bekker

First Edition 1993

Cover graphic by
Heidi Lange

Reproduction by Multigraphics
Printed by The Natal Witness
Printing and Publishing Co (Pty) Ltd

ISBN: 1 - 86840 - 054 - 9

The INDICATOR SOUTH AFRICA Issue Focus series is published by the
Centre for Social and Development Studies at the University of Natal.

TABLE OF CONTENTS

PREFACE

Simon Bekker's book is both re-assuring and disconcerting. Its thoroughness, skill in dealing with complexity and the balanced judgment it reveals are a reminder that social scientists have a role to play in helping a troubled and complicated society to understand itself. It is disconcerting in that it provides a massive accumulation of evidence that many more than two generations of social scientists have worked very hard to miss the point.

Poincaré described sociology as '... the science with the greatest number of methods and the least results'. Simon Bekker's review of the study of ethnicity in South Africa seems to confirm that sarcasm. He takes us through a large assembly of authors who wrote millions of words to attempt to show either that an inevitable, categorical cultural identity transcends all other interests, that it is merely a kind of artificial social consciousness manipulated into prominence to serve or disguise class interests or that it is a traditional self-categorisation that individuals will discard as they become liberated by education, occupational pursuits or modern urban life. After reading Bekker's review I could not help asking myself whether an ordinary housewife or the owner of a hot-dog stand, in 1970, 1980, 1990, would not have had the wisdom to say that ethnicity can be a bit of everything.

Bekker shows how authors, in their search for the more fundamental realities, from three or more major points of view concluded that observable consistencies in behaviour around them, had to be denied and explained away. The book therefore, is first and foremost perhaps a plea for intellectual honesty.

It is more than that, however. It also attempts to show that underneath the horrors and crudity of apartheid, there were processes common to virtually all other societies which would survive apartheid, class struggle, national liberation and socio-economic development. It suggests that one of the most damaging of apartheid's effects was to produce an intellectual arthritis, among both its supporters and opponents.

Finally it deals very thoroughly with the hypothesis of the hypothesis of the housewife and the hot-dog merchant, in teasing out the different levels of ethnic consciousness and the way it interacts with, is part of, yet conceptually separate from, other divisions in our society. It is identity, but it also becomes structured and collectivised as community and, being pervasive and emotive, can be mobilised to serve the ends of power and privilege.

I finished reading the book with the feeling that Simon Bekker would help us all to be courageous enough to take our society more seriously, and be a little less inclined to use it as a way of confirming our prior commitments.

We obviously need all the help we can get because, tragically, so-called race and ethnic relations today, on the threshold of liberation from apartheid, are possibly more troubled than they have been ever before. Lives are being lost at the rate of over ten per day in political violence. Private armies on the right and left are mobilising under ethnic or racial banners. Our current recession has been hopelessly prolonged by the political instability.

Let us hope therefore, that the research and scholarship in this time of troubled transition will not, as before, try to prove that the dynamics of our turmoil are to be found in obscure linkages with fundamentals which are beyond our ability to deal with. After reading Bekker's review, I hope that we will not be taken through tortuous logic to 'prove' that this or that category of people can never accept an open democracy, or that some or another category of violence is being manipulated by corporate capital, that 'third forces' are so omnipotent that they can control thousands of people like puppets or that if we intone 'non-racial, non-sexist democracy' often enough in learned articles it will somehow materialise.

If we as social scientists are going to help South Africa overcome its past, we must be prepared to confront a muddled reality, riddled with history and often driven by consciousnesses we would dearly love to call 'false'. If we respect South Africa's people we must, in addition to the underlying factors we would assert, respect their definitions and consciousnesses. This, I detect, is what Simon Bekker is saying to us.

LAWRENCE SCHLEMMER
Vice President, Human Sciences Research Council

ACKNOWLEDGEMENTS

This study was completed in 1993. Most of the work was undertaken during a five month period of study leave which I spent as a visiting Fellow of the Centre d'Étude d'Afrique Noire (CEAN) at Bordeaux in France. I would like to thank my colleagues at CEAN for their hospitality and support. I would also like to acknowledge the influence of French intellectual thought on my work.

There is a story told about the German novelist, Lion Feuchtwanger, who was met by a group of American journalists in New York City after leaving Germany for the United States in the early 1940s. He was asked whether he liked Americans. 'No', he replied. He was asked whether he liked Germans. 'No', he repeated. He was then asked whom it was that he did like. 'My friends', he replied.

This study uses as its main sources the scholarly works of my colleagues and my friends. In criticizing them, I do not wish to create the impression that these works are deeply flawed or of little value. Scholarship on modern South Africa is extraordinary in reflecting quality, dedication, and - often - courage. My purpose is to show that this community of scholars faces new challenges and needs new currents of thought to tackle them.

For criticisms of drafts of this study, I would like to thank Catherine Cross, Dominique Darbon, Jim Kiernan, Jeffery Lever, Denis-Constant Martin, David Seymour, John Sharp, Gavin Williams, and John Wright.

I would also like to express grateful acknowledgment to the University of Natal and to the Ernest Oppenheimer Memorial Trust for financial support during this period, and to the Division of Human Rights and Peace of Unesco for a grant to complete a study on ethnicity and democracy.

Simon Bekker   December 1993

Note: No analysis of ethnicity in contemporary South African society is able to escape terminological dilemmas. I have decided to use the term 'Black' in an inclusive sense, to include the predominantly Bantu-speaking 'African' majority, and the 'Coloured' and 'Indian' categories. I will also use the term, 'White' to refer to members of that erstwhile officially designated category. By using this terminology, I do not intend to imply any necessary form of mutually experienced identity or community consciousness. I will use the term, group where such solidarity does exist, and the term, category where such solidarity is not apparent.

'How am I able to know that which I am about to say?'
('Comment puis-je savoir ce que je vais dire?')
Marc Bloch *Apologie pour l'histoire* 1949.

INTRODUCTION

Astonishing though it may seem to most rank-and-file South Africans, there is little discussion on ethnicity in South Africa at the moment. It is an issue not raised during public political negotiations, nor addressed in development interventions, nor discussed during most scholarly debates. It is not considered to be important.

Elsewhere, the issue is confused. Though often considered important - and, accordingly, acknowledged by governments, recognised by development agencies, debated by scholars, and sometimes built into constitutions - there are wide disagreements about what ethnicity is, about how and when it emerges, and about what can and ought to be done about it. In contemporary social science, it is probably the greatest enigma of our time.

I have chosen four recent claims regarding the importance of the issue in South Africa to illustrate its enigmatic nature. Each claim is made by a highly experienced and widely respected scholar: the first two are internationally recognised; the latter two, well-known in South Africa.

Writing in the late 1980s, Claude Meillassoux, a French anthropologist and historian with wide African experience, claims that African communities in the country, 'confined in the reserves or in dormitory suburbs which service white cities, have experienced social mixing as a result of state manipulation which in effect means that contemporary "ethnic groups" in South Africa are no more than administrative inventions, without historical foundations or living social identities'[1].

After a revisit to South Africa in 1989, Pierre van den Berghe who has studied numerous plural societies, including South African society in the 1960s[2], makes the following assertions:

> South Africa remains a plural society with a population divided by deep rifts of class, race, and ethnicity. I see no clear evidence that those rifts have diminished over the last three decades...
>
> I consider it highly likely that race and ethnicity will continue to play a salient role in South African politics for the foreseeable future, with probably a decreasing emphasis on race and an increasing one on ethnicity (based on language). (van den Berghe 1990: 17, 36)

In 1992, Marinus Wiechers, professor of constitutional law at the University of South Africa, writes:

> ... a person from a certain race group with a specific background will almost inevitably, as a result of that racial adherence and background, be predisposed to practice the dominant culture, language and religion of the group to which he belongs. Even in a very advanced or individualised society, ethnic change or transfer occurs seldom. With very few exceptions, modern legal systems have achieved little more than to ensure that members of ethnic groups are not discriminated against on account of their ethnic qualities. (Wiechers 1992: 1)

As a fourth illustration, I have selected the following analysis proposed by Paulus Zulu, a well-known South African sociologist:

> Successive (South African) governments ruled Africans as a common group and no distinct regional or ethnic groupings mobilised against white rule on any significant ethnic 'ticket'. Liberation movements such as the ANC and the PAC organised on a non-ethnic or non-racial basis. It was the National Party that created and rewarded politicised ethnicity in order to sustain it. Cleavages which arise out of this form of social engineering are, therefore, not natural but contrived... (Zulu 1992: 27)

The purpose of this book is to show, in contemporary South Africa, that ethnicity, in its various forms, is important, that *questions* about ethnicity ought to be debated. On the evidence, I am not convinced by those that argue that the issue will remain a non-issue in the future. Equally, I am not convinced by those who argue that ethnicity will become the major salient political challenge in South Africa's future. I *am* convinced that we need more evidence: more understanding of what ethnicity is, of how and why it manifests itself at different times and in other countries. Most importantly, we need to understand the changing multiple identities of themselves and changing images of their communities and of their society which ordinary South Africans are creating. We then need to debate this evidence with a view to recognising and appreciating the cultural diversity of the country, and with a view to avoiding potential conflicts arising from this diversity. Finally, since the current profound changes both in the country and internationally are, in a sense, going to 'produce' a 'new' South Africa in a 'new' global dispensation, debating such ethnic questions may enable South Africa's constitutional and social engineers together with its citizenry to 'produce' a better society.

To achieve this purpose, I will call on the knowledge and wisdom of a range of international scholars. I will discuss the notion of ethnicity, primarily by using this knowledge and wisdom of international scholars. I will show that this community of scholars agree on the importance of the issue while sharing little more than generalities and programmatic statements in their search for explanations for the occurrence of ethnic phenomena. A satisfactory scholarly understanding of ethnicity has yet to be developed and the ideas and theories presently employed appear to be primitive.

Subsequently, I will explain why such questions, of late, have virtually disappeared from most influential scholarly debates on South African society. More specifically, I will show and attempt to explain why, over the last fifteen years, scholarly works on South Africa - largely produced by South Africans - have disregarded these questions. Instead, they have employed representations of South African society constructed on the basis of theories which use other ideas, those of race, class, nationalism, and state in particular. And by so doing, these scholars have argued that the identities and images of their society which South Africans possess are predominantly structured by these ideas, by their racial classification, by their class position, by their adherence to nationalist ideologies, and by their relationship to the South African state. Being South African, these scholars implied, meant being different; different within their society as a result of imposed state and economic divisions, and, accordingly, different from people living in other societies since their society was particularly divergent.

Only rarely have ethnic identity and the existence of ethnic community been addressed, without an adequate conceptual framework and typically as an epiphenomenon. The one major exception, the representation of South African society as 'a vertical division between equal ethnic groups or nations' was none other than the ideology of apartheid, an ideology - not a scholarly representation - which was regarded from its inception some fifty years ago as unacceptable by most South African scholars and one which, by 1976, had also been rejected by most Afrikaner nationalist scholars[3].

I will conclude with a short analysis of the challenges facing South African scholarship during the contemporary phase of transition in South Africa. Two contemporary sets of circumstances will guide this analysis. Recent events in the country, specifically the persisting cycles of political and communal violence and the extended process of national constitutional negotiations, have focused public attention on ethnic identities, ethnic communities, and the potential for ethnic mobilisation. As a result, there appears to be tentative, renewed interest in the subject. Three recent scholarly conferences attest to this trend[4].

In the second place, a new international global order is being established. Everywhere, the old order of Western and Eastern blocs, of capitalist and communist ideologies, of Third World countries as pawns caught up in the Cold War, is disappearing. As a consequence, numerous nation-states are reacting defensively as local politics and global politics increasingly articulate similar demands, for human and cultural rights and for equity in access to resources. These demands act as incentives for emergent groups within these societies to assert their differences, to assert the uniqueness they experience, in contradistinction to other groups within the same society. It is probable that many South Africans will - in time - see themselves and, accordingly, find themselves within this new emerging world order.

NOTES
1. Meillassoux 1988: 14. My translation.
2. van den Berghe 1964, 1967.
3. Giliomee and Schlemmer 1989b: Ch 2.
4. The first conference, entitled Ethnicity, Society and Conflict in Natal, took place at the University of Natal, Pietermaritzburg in September 1992; the second, entitled, État, Nation, Ethnicité, took place at the Centre d'Étude d'Afrique Noire, Bordeaux, France in November 1992; and the third, entitled Ethnicity, Identity and Nationalism in South Africa: Comparative Perspectives, took place at Rhodes University, Grahamstown in April 1993.

II A COMPARATIVE VIEW OF ETHNICITY

Ethnicity... is a phenomenon that is, in ways not yet explicated, no mere survival but intimately and organically bound up with major trends of modern societies. (Glazer and Moynihan 1975: 26)

In the foreword to a 1991 report entitled 'Research on Ethnicity' produced by the Woodrow Wilson International Center for Scholars, its director writes: 'It is surely unnecessary at this moment in history to spend time justifying the importance of a more perfect understanding of the phenomenon - or phenomena - known as "ethnicity"'[1]. It has become standard practice, among many scholars and analysts of modern plural societies (societies which are variously called 'divided', 'culturally heterogeneous', 'multi-ethnic' or 'multi-communal'), to interpret social and political movements in ethnic terms.

It is appropriate to start with a number of examples which illustrate the degree to which the existence and importance of this issue is commonly recognised. Though the terminology is not always the same, strikingly similar general conclusions drawn from six sources, written by scholars who share neither the same theoretical approach nor the same substantive interests, will be presented.

The sources are all recent and comparative, each dealing with a number of contemporary societies. The first two claim to have a general relevance in non-Western plural societies, the third focuses on Eastern Europe, the fourth on the Third World, and the fifth and sixth on Africa.

Drawing on a wide range of work, particularly in Asia, Africa and the Caribbean, Horowitz asserts that:

> In divided societies, ethnic conflict is at the center of politics. Ethnic divisions pose challenges to the cohesion of states and sometimes to peaceful relations among states. Ethnic conflict strains the bonds that sustain civility and is often at the root of violence that results in looting, death, homelessness, and the flight of large numbers of people. In divided societies, ethnic affiliations are powerful, permeative, passionate, and pervasive. (Horowitz 1985:12)

This argument is somewhat circular since the divided nature of these societies appears to imply the potential for ethnic conflict. Later in the same work, he points to:

> the commonly held notion in the early years after independence that there was a need for a massive shift of loyalties from the ethnic group to the state in the interests of 'nation-building'. The assumption was that ethnic loyalties subsisted at a lower level and lagged behind the development of the modern state. What we have seen shows this assumption to be unfounded. More often than not, ethnic groups are the product of altered levels of loyalty and are already keyed to the state level. (Ibid: 82)

Theo Hanf of the Arnold Bergstraesser Institute in Germany, uses a 'plural society' conceptual scheme[2] when he argues as follows:

> Theories of modernization postulate that industrialization, urbanisation and communication are powerful forces for social integration and would rapidly break down communal loyalties. In practice, the realities of social development in multi-communal societies have for the most part refuted this assumption. Although people from different communities live together in the new cities, they do not necessarily mix. Their contact is for the most part in competing for jobs and posts in industry and the public administration. In this competitive situation they receive assistance and patronage primarily from their immediate compatriots, their fellow tribesmen and fellow speakers, in short: communal support... But perhaps of even greater importance, they frequently experience inequality, rejection and discrimination as a result of the ascriptive criteria of their community affiliation. Social inequality is a powerful revitaliser of communal solidarity. (1989: 101)

Professor Miroslav Kusy, president of the former Czechoslovak committee of the European Cultural Foundation, identified the importance of self-conscious minorities when he analysed the situation in Eastern Europe (in 1991) in the following way:

> The problem of minorities is not an isolated problem, it does not arise by itself, and neither does it exist by itself. It is the product of a certain situational social context. It arises (out of) the relationship of a minority towards a majority, a national and ethnic minority toward 'the state-forming nation' The disintegration of power structures in Eastern Europe... stimulates (such) processes...
>
> The totalitarian regimes have up to now neglected (such) political rights of nations... Now, after the fall of the totalitarian regimes, comes their chance... (a) basic impulse... (toward) real-to-life politics. Their efforts are unambiguous: political rights of the 'state-forming nations' have to be compensated for by similar political rights of national and ethnic minorities'.
> (Bratislava Symposium 1991: 19)

In a paper written for Unesco on ethnicity, development and democracy, three scholars (two based in Switzerland and one in Hong Kong) declare as follows:

> Of all the factors that influence the social and political systems of Third World countries, none perhaps is more important than ethnicity. The very future of some countries as united sovereign states is in doubt due to ethnic conflicts. In many others, political order is difficult to establish and social and economic developments are bedeviled by ethnic differences. In many parts of the globe, ethnic minorities suffer appalling discrimination and live in fear. Ethnic conflicts frequently spill over across state boundaries and threaten international peace. The correct and creative handling of the tensions and conflicts which arise from ethnic differences has become a supreme test of statesmanship in most countries of the world, particularly in the Third World.
>
> (Ghai *et al*. 1992: 80)

The fifth example is taken from the conclusion of a book written in 1990 on the failure of the centralised state in Africa. It attempts to generalise across a number of different societies:

> To understand the political path Africa's leaders have followed, one must note (a factor) which (was) particularly disturbing to African leaders and modernization scholars: the large number of ethnic groups brought together by the accident of colonial rule...
>
> One of the key goals of modernization was the integration of these diverse ethnic groups (condescendingly referred to as tribes) through the imposition of the dominant culture of the modernizing elite: intellectuals, senior civil servants, and political officials...
>
> While some states have fared better in institutionalizing stable representation of key groups at the center (Senegal, Kenya), others have not, and at times intense conflict has been the result (Ghana, Nigeria, Uganda, Sudan). Highly centralized states with little institutionalization of rules of accession, representation and secession, are an explosive combination. Within such a system, disadvantaged groups have few options other than secession bids, as in the Sudan, Ethiopia, Chad, and Biafra in the late 60s. At times this has led to open warfare. (Wunsch and Olowu: 304, 307)

Finally, in a 1991 article published in the Review of African Political Economy, Doornbos cautiously suggests that:

> In Africa... ethnicity... figures, and is perceived to figure, as one basic constitutive element prevalent in and throughout virtually all societies, essentially underscoring how, in one respect, the social fabric of most African countries is made up from a fairly complex and to some extent fluid ensemble of different people, nations and nationalities, ethnic strata and in some cases caste-like divisions. (Doornbos 1991: 58, 59)

Two observations about this brief survey need immediately to be made. The first is that such a survey does not enable us to anticipate what will happen in comparable societies or regions. 'It would be quite misleading to interpret and use results of particular comparative studies as a reliable basis for predictions in analogous situations'[3]. This is so since explanations for the emergence and persistence of ethnic movements remain visibly incomplete. Wide variations across case studies regarding demography, economic circumstances, ethnic manipulation, political systems, and - probably most importantly - histories, render attempts to predict highly speculative. Consider the following argument in a recent Unesco publication:

> As a source of conflict, ethnicity takes its coloration from the specific circumstances of time and society. It is difficult to pin it down as an independent variable in the ordering of social, political and economic life... Ethnicity is (also) highly manipulable: indeed its very existence can be conjured out of vague bonds and symbols of association. There is a dynamic quality to ethnic relations which suggests that more attention should be paid to history than is customary in the study of ethnic relations. (Ghai *et al.* 1992: 81)

Such difficulties regarding comparability have led some scholars to narrow their frames of reference, to limit the context within which comparison takes place. In order to attempt to 'remedy this situation', Vail claims to have located 'the study of ethnicity within the unfolding history of a set of societies (in Southern Africa) which are *genuinely* comparable'[4]. In like vein, Doornbos appeals for 'the need to understand ethnicity in context (which) requires a proper grasp of the specificity of its configuration in the African case, as compared... to its occurrence (elsewhere)'[5]. In both cases, the authors claim that their narrower territorial contexts share some (but only some) historical experience.

The second observation relates to the tentative nature of many of the generalisations made about ethnicity. It is worth noting that all of the scholars quoted above qualify their assertions: 'perhaps', 'for the most part', 'more often than not', 'virtually, 'in one respect' are examples.

These two observations are clearly related. If satisfactory theory and reliable information are insufficient and if it is difficult, accordingly, to predict outcomes in comparable circumstances and situations, it is equally difficult to reach reasonable certainty regarding generalisations. In fact, adequate understanding and reasonable anticipation of outcomes may be even more difficult: 'Part of the explanation for the many shortcomings in our understanding of ethnicity is the episodic character of ethnic conflict itself. It comes and goes, suddenly shattering periods of apparent tranquillity. The suddenness of the phenomenon helps explain the lag in understanding it. As scholarship is reactive, the spilling of ink awaits the spilling of blood'[6].

What such a survey *does* enable us to do is to ask specific questions about a comparable society. Doubtless, any reader with South Africa in mind will have examined recent histories of this society in the light of the generalisations made by the scholars cited above, and will have found some that seem to ring true and others false.

Let us turn therefore to the question of South African society. Let us first discuss the notion of ethnicity as it may apply to South Africa. In particular, let us attempt to distinguish between this notion and three other ideas which have been particularly influential in the analysis of modern South African society. We will then be able to ask whether this society has developed in ways so different from those touched upon above that most of the generalisations made are of little use to South African scholars. Such a decision would be an important one to make since the assertions made above are of profound importance to those societies.

NOTES

1. Blitzer 1991: 5.
2. See the section on sociology and political science in Ch. VI for a discussion of the plural society approach.
3. Hanf 1989: 89.
4. Vail 1989b: 7. My emphasis.
5. Doornbos 1991: 58.
6. Horowitz 1985:13.

ETHNICITY AND SOUTH AFRICA

*(T)he definition of the ethnic group studied should form the
fundamental epistemological enquiry in any scholarly monograph,
from which the other aspects should flow.*
(Amselle and M'Bokolo 1985: 11 My translation)

Discussing ethnicity

Over the past two decades, ethnicity has been addressed by numerous scholars
throughout the world. As used in their analyses, the concept has remained
profoundly indistinct. Its use varies according to the disciplinary background
of the scholars, according to the social, cultural, and historical problems they
investigate, and according to their differing ideological convictions[1]. It is - as
I proposed earlier - fundamentally enigmatic.

What I intend to do here is to discuss the notion of ethnicity. I will use the works
of international scholars to guide the discussion and will keep South African
society in mind to focus the discussion. The nature of this society is deeply
contested by different scholars, as will be shown below, and life in this society
is experienced in deeply different ways by different groups and categories of
South Africans. Nonetheless, it is generally agreed that modern South Africa
is a plural society in which these different groups and categories have
experienced division along lines, *inter alia*, of language (for over 200 years
during which various languages changed, merged, were codified, and took
root), of territory (before the twentieth century in separate pre-colonial and
settler societies, and after, under different state-imposed dispensations) and of
changing relationships to the South African state and to the economy of the
country.

There are numerous ways to approach such a discussion. Ethnicity has been
conceptualised as embedded in culture and values, as emerging from common
networks and institutions, and as arising from communal and political interests.
I will touch on these approaches in the discussion. The main approach I have
decided to employ is to view ethnicity at two levels. The advantage of this
approach is that it distinguishes, in modern plural societies like South Africa,

between the probable, episodic and changing nature of ethnicity at the level of individual identity, and the probable persistence of ethnic allegiances at the level of community. By using such a distinction, the approach then leads us to questions about the relationship between these two levels, and accordingly, to questions about the potential for ethnic conflicts and ethnic changes in such plural societies. It also points to a path between a purely social constructivist view of ethnicity which emphasizes the invented, imagined and malleable nature of ethnic identity, and a purely primordialist one which emphasizes the fixity of ethnic definition.

It is useful, accordingly, to begin by pointing to two levels of ethnicity. The first refers to individuals and ethnic identity. This level raises questions regarding socialisation and education, ethnogenesis at the level of the individual, identity as 'narrative', and other social psychological issues. It is also a level at which stereotypes may be, and often are, studied[2]. It is a crucial dimension, but one that cannot, on its own, be used to discuss ethnicity in South Africa comprehensively. In this regard, Roosens writes:

> In the elasticity of the expression 'ethnic identity', the dynamic character of the cultural, the social, and the psychological becomes visible in combination... The term 'ethnic identity' can, for example, refer to origin, uniqueness, passing on of life, 'blood', solidarity, unity, security, personal integrity, independence, recognition, equality, cultural uniqueness, respect, equal economic rights, territorial integrity, and so on... *It is impossible for ethnic identity to mean anything without the existence of ethnic groups or categories*, for it is a relational construct. (Roosens 1989: 19. My emphasis.)

The second level refers to ethnic communities. Anthony Smith uses the French term *ethnie*, 'which unites an emphasis upon cultural differences with a sense of an historical community'. He then lists six dimensions of an ethnic community: a collective name, a common myth of descent, a shared history, a distinctive shared culture, an association with a specific territory, and a sense of solidarity.[3] Some years later, he defines ethnic communities as 'collective cultural units claiming common ancestry, shared memories and symbols, whether they constitute majorities or minorities in a given state'[4].

This level raises questions regarding the cultural ideas and consciousness, and the histories of these communities. It points to continuity - to inter-generational ties and to shared memories - in ethnic communities whereas the first level, the manner of identification by an individual who belongs to (or chooses to belong to) such an ethnic community, points rather to flux, to choice between multiple identities available to him or to her in different socio-economic and political contexts:

> By fixing attention mainly on the great dimensions and 'fault lines' of religion, customs, language, and institutions, we run the risk of treating ethnicity as something primordial and fixed. By concentrating solely on the attitudes and sentiments and political movements of fixed *ethnie* or ethnic fragments, we risk being so caught up in the day-to-day ebb and flow of ethnic phenomena that we see them as wholly dependent 'tools' or 'boundary markers' of other social and economic forces. (Smith 1986: 211)

So far, both these levels have been considered in relation to a single ethnic community, to a 'cultural isolate' as it were. This perspective is unwarranted, and, for South African society at least, highly dangerous for it conjures up outdated anthropological, and more contemporary (apartheid-related) ideological, ideas about African (and Afrikaner) 'tribes' and 'nations'. In plural societies, one form of ethnicity needs to be considered in relation to other forms of ethnicity, or, at the first level, in relation to other forms of (possibly non-ethnic) identity. 'An ethnic group only makes sense with reference to other groups, most of them also ethnic. Conceptually, ethnicity subverts the platonic autonomy of the isolate tribe, just as the state may threaten its physical existence'[5]. A study of ethnicity, accordingly, involves simultaneously an analysis of individual identities and their genesis in a plural society, and an historical analysis of the origins and elaboration of the different and changing ethnic consciousnesses which mould or influence these identities. In Crawford Young's words: 'The necessity to weave together the instrumentalist and the primordialist dimensions of ethnicity is self-evident'[6].

Accordingly, it is clear that a discussion of ethnicity needs to address not only socio-economic and political issues, but also cultural ones. Three relevant analyses which illustrate the inter-relationship between socio-economic, political and cultural issues will now be given.

To Denis Martin, in an article which calls for a deeper understanding of 'moral pluralism' in developing countries, culture includes, as an essential component, a system of values, 'a code through which the ethical orientation of a particular society (or community) relates to its institutions and its structure of authority'[7]. After typifying cultures as changing rather than fixed, he identifies individualism as a central value in modern European societies and then argues that:

> In Asia and in Africa the individual has never been totally freed from the

community. The ideological permanence and power of links between people and communities in many non-European societies cannot be underestimated and they undoubtedly influence the ethical orientations of these societies... Another area in which European and indigenous norms clash relates to the persistence of the family as the focus of daily social and economic life in Africa.

African contemporary societies now accommodate unique balances between individuals and communities, between competition and solidarity. (1991: 328,331,332)

In like vein, Horowitz claims that:

The power and permeativeness of ethnicity in the developing world owe much to the considerable strength of kinship ties in Asia and Africa. In the West, most tasks outside the home are performed by organizations not based on kinship. The same is simply not true in Asia and Africa or is only accurate with a great deal of qualification, recognizing that formally impersonal institutions are actually infused with personal considerations of several kinds; and this is particularly the case with kinship. Reciprocally, the need and expectation of help strengthen the bonds of the extended family. They are ties it pays to keep in good order. In the West, on the other hand, the expectation that impersonal criteria will generally (though not always) be applied to formally impersonal transactions weakens the ties of extended kinship. Conversely, the nuclear family strengthens the role of impersonal criteria. (1985: 63)

In a collected study of the recent histories of Southern African societies, Vail claims that 'the (Witwatersrand's)[8] influence was everywhere present, if only as a model of labour relations and a distant and powerful, economic presence. Although certainly uneven, the Rand's influence knitted the region's territories together'. He then argues that:

one of the most far-reaching and important new forms of consciousness (to emerge) was a new ethnic - or tribal - consciousness that could and did encapsulate other forms of consciousness. Ethnicity could coexist with other types of consciousness without apparent unease because *it was cultural and hence based on involuntary ascription, not on personal choice.* People were members of a particular ethnic group whether they liked it or not. It was simply a fact of existence. As such, ethnic identity could inhere in both petty bourgeois and worker, in both peasant farmer and striving politician. (1989b: 8,10. My emphasis)

It would seem, accordingly, that only through a sustained historical analysis of socio-economic, political and cultural issues, on both levels of ethnicity, is the complexity of ethnic relationships captured.

Both levels are clearly relevant to an analysis of modern South Africa. In particular, the deeply plural nature of this society raises sharply a question regarding the potential for ethnic conflicts. As Avruch puts it:

> Ethnicity connotes conflict because it brings groups together in the same arenas; both materially, under a state in competition for resources and power, and conceptually, as part of a shared universe of discourse - and discord. (Avruch 1992: 616)

In more historical vein, Horowitz writes:

> Certain worldwide ideological and institutional currents have... underpinned the growth of ethnic conflict. The spread of norms of equality has made ethnic subordination illegitimate and spurred ethnic groups everywhere to compare their standing in society against that of groups in close proximity. The simultaneous spread of the value of achievement has cast in doubt (and in self-doubt) the worth of groups whose competitive performance seems deficient by such standards. (Horowitz 1985: 5)

Appropriately for South African society, ethnicity is considered, in these two quotations, to be embedded in the context of a single state[9]. Under such a condition, Davis observes that '(e)thnic identity is a claim against government for recognition and special treatment, and it is cast as a history'[10].

Also appropriate for South Africa is the observation that ethnic conflicts are related to perceived group inequality within a single state. This relationship - between ethnic conflicts and perceived group inequality - is recognised virtually universally in the modern literature on ethnicity[11].

An analysis of this relationship, however, which focuses solely on the first level - the identity level - of ethnicity tends to treat such identities as epiphenomenonal, in Smith's words, 'as wholly dependent "tools" or "boundary markers" of other social and economic forces'. Such studies often use a materialist form of analysis and seek to demonstrate a primary consciousness rooted in economic and political conditions. Horowitz, in his 1985 survey of ethnic conflict in Third World societies, is direct and frank in his criticism of this form of analysis:

> (E)conomic theories cannot explain the extent of the emotion invested in ethnic conflict... (M)aterialist theories leave unexplained the striving for such goals as domination (or autonomy), a 'legitimate place in the country', and 'the symbols of prestige', all of which may take precedence over economic interests in determining group behavior. (Horowitz: 134,135)

With regard to ethnic conflict and its resolution, he then goes on to argue:

> This much however is very clear. Symbolic claims are not readily amenable to compromise. In this, they differ from claims deriving wholly from material interests. Whereas material advancement can be measured both relatively and absolutely, the status advancement of one ethnic group is entirely relative to the status of others. That is an important reason for being precise about what is at stake in ethnic conflict. Ethnic claims are expressed in moral language and are not quantifiable... (223,224)

A focus on potential ethnic conflicts raises the question of the changing political organisations and programmes of ethnic communities. It is clear that the role of ethnic elites (variously called ethnic 'entrepreneurs', 'brokers', or 'manipulators')[12] is critical to this process of mobilisation. The process is an interactive one, with members of the community defining the outlines of a programme, and leaders and elites refining these outlines and specifying political claims. Bates, for example, argues that '(e)thnic groups are able to extract investments from persons seeking access to elite positions in the "modern" order. Moreover, the "moderns" need, and seek to elicit, the support of ethnic groupings'[13]. On the other hand, '(p)olitical leaders can create stereotypes that give almost religious exaltedness to ethnic identity (which), via stereotypes, lead to economic and cultural wars with other groups...'[14]. There is accordingly continuing tension between the identification and selection of ethnic elites, on the one hand, and the manipulation and mobilisation by ethnic elites, on the other; between the reproduction, re-invention and reconstruction of ethnicity, as it were; between continuity and flux. It is only through empirical analysis of each specific case that adequate understanding may be reached.

It is prudent, at this point in the discussion, to pause and inquire whether what we have learnt from scholars studying plural societies other than South Africa is of use to scholars of South Africa. Is it plausible to inquire whether modern South African society, in fundamental transition during the 1990s, contains within itself various ethnic communities with which large numbers of citizens are identifying in different and changing ways? Is it plausible to ask, in so far as these forms of identification are taking place, why this is so? What forms of ethnic consciousness and of ethnic mobilisation are emerging? Is it plausible to ask, again in reference to the experience of other plural societies, what potential for ethnic conflicts there is in this plural society? What emergent forms this conflict is taking on, and why?

There is a real danger in posing such general questions which focus *solely* on ethnicity. As we saw in Chapter II, a number of scholars have warned against using generalisations in studies of particular societies. Some pleaded for a narrower frame of reference, for more adequate contextualisation, before ethnicity is addressed. As we have seen in this chapter, moreover, a number of scholars have also pointed to the essentially relational nature of ethnicity, relational both regarding other ethnic consciousnesses in a plural society, and relational regarding, particularly, perceived group inequalities in a plural society. It is necessary, accordingly, to focus our discussion by locating it more squarely within modern South African society.

Distinguishing between crucial ideas

It is common knowledge to most members of modern South African society that profound material inequalities coincide in large part with 'race' classifications in their society. Thus, as many scholars maintain, different classes have emerged from urban-industrial economic development in modern South Africa and these classes largely coincide with different racial categories. In addition, it is widely accepted that 'nationalism' - particularly Afrikaner nationalism - has played an important role in creating this society. In which ways do racial, class, and national 'identities'; racial 'communities', classes, and national 'communities'; differ from ethnic identities and ethnic communities?

Race

The idea of 'race' has played a central role in scholarly analyses of modern South Africa. Rooted in earlier European systems of thought[15]. it took on different meanings among different groups at different times in South Africa[16]. Consider the following two claims:

> Color is the sole determinant of power in South Africa. (This power) not only provides for the whites' security, but also enables them to retain their position of economic and social privilege over a colored majority... Security and the maintenance of privilege are held to be inseparable. (Legum 1967: 483)

> There is a conflict in South Africa that has something to do with race. That is about as far as agreement runs among many of the participants and interpreters

of the conflict. Beyond that, there is disagreement over the extent to which the conflict is really *about* race, as opposed to being about oppression merely in the guise of race, or about nationalism among groups demarcated by race, or about contending claims to the same land.
(Horowitz 1991a: 1. Emphasis in the original)

Though modern scholars are in agreement that 'races' - '(group) differences based on physical or morphological characteristics' - are social and cultural constructs, they disagree on whether socially relevant differences of this nature should be distinguished from socially relevant differences based on other criteria (such as '"tribal", linguistic, national, religious or other cultural characteristics'[17]). Horowitz argues that those who do claim that a significant distinction needs to be drawn between 'racial' conflict and 'ethnic' conflict confuse the indicator of the relationship - colour, in the first place, and other non-physical cultural criteria, in the second - for the substance of the relationship[18]. He introduces the idea of ranked and unranked ethnic groups to explain this substance:

> The distinction rests upon the coincidence or non coincidence of social class with ethnic origins. When the two coincide, it is possible to speak of ranked ethnic groups, where groups are cross-class, it is possible to speak of unranked ethnic groups. This distinction is as fundamental as it is neglected. (1985: 21,22)

Scholars who claim that racial conflict differs from other forms of ethnic conflicts are dealing with ranked ethnic groups in societies which have developed systems of racial categorisation largely coinciding with system of group stratification, in societies within which 'the historical association of color differences with subordination and the conflict-laden efforts to overcome it'[19] have become primary. It is as a consequence of the history and circumstances of these societies, not of the racial constructs and beliefs themselves, that racial conflict appears to be different from other forms of ethnic conflicts.

This implies an inclusive notion of ethnicity which includes perceived group differences identified not only by language, by religion, or by some other (non-physical) characteristics common to the group, but also by colour. Colour ('race') tends to become an important indicator or marker of group difference in societies where class differences and colour differences have come to overlap, in other words, in societies including ranked ethnic groups. The fact that perceived race may arouse intense emotions and is often viewed as indelible and immutable, has led some scholars to distinguish between ethnic and racial groups in principle, but counter-examples in these regards[20] as well as the advantage of comparative analysis justify the more inclusive notion of ethnicity.

The distinction between ranked and unranked ethnic groups is useful. Other scholars use it[21]. With regard to modern South African society, it enables an ethnic analysis of the Afrikaner category, for instance, which will differ from ethnic analyses of the apartheid-subordinated Black, African, Coloured, Indian, and intra-African categories.

It also enables a distinction to be drawn in South African society between statutory racial classification - a form of state-imposed ethnic stratification - and individual and group rejection of, or identification with, this system of racial stratification. In other words, 'race' in modern South African society needs to be analysed along two separate dimensions. The first is that of the statutory imposition of racial classification on all South Africans by a White minority government (together with the history leading up to, and subsequently elaborating, this system of racial classification and concomitant racial stratification). The second concerns the identity-related consequences which this system has had on different South African groups and categories. Adam and Moodley recognise these two dimensions when they write:

> (Racial) identification is lacking among all spokespersons of the non-White population, who, on the contrary, reject racial labeling. The very need for legislation for four racial groups testifies to the non-voluntary nature of the groupings. Ironically, in South Africa the official racial categorization has contributed to the rejection of ethnic boundaries that perhaps would otherwise have been supported voluntarily. (1986: 16)

As South African society moves away from a system of state-imposed racial classification, the potential for individual and group identification with indicators other than race will probably increase. Simultaneously, since the current system of stratification will not disappear simply as a result of the removal of racial statutes, forms of racial identification and consciousness will probably persist for a substantial period.

Class

On first sight, the ideas of class identity and of class itself - a class community - seem self-evident, and the ways they differ from ethnic identity and ethnic community obvious. Thus, a modern urban-industrial society like South Africa, a capitalist society[22], develops a middle class, a bourgeoisie, and a working class, a proletariat. Classes are defined by the relationship their members have to the common economic system of the society. Members of the working class, for instance, share 'a common lack of either ownership or control of the means of production'[23]. A class category, 'a class in itself', points to a collectivity of people who do not share the same felt economic interests. On the other hand, a class community, 'a class for itself', is one where common class interests are shared, where a class consciousness has developed. Class identity, accordingly, points to identification with these common interests, identification with this class consciousness.

The complex theoretical debates on the roles which such classes play in modern urban industrial societies need not concern us here. They will be discussed in the next chapter. What is of direct concern, however, is the distinction between class identity and ethnic identity, and between a class and an ethnic community.

One way to approach the question is to start with Anthony Smith's definition of ethnic communities: 'collective cultural units claiming common ancestry, shared memories and symbols, whether they constitute majorities or minorities in a given state'[24]. In so far as a class tends to fit this definition, by claims to a common working class culture, for example, and to working class parents and grandparents (though this differs from common ancestry), and to a shared working class history, may it then be compared to an ethnic community? And if so, in how far are some ethnic communities simply masks for classes, for class communities; and in how far is some ethnic conflict simply a manifestation of class conflict?

In the first place, answers given to such questions must be empirical, involving analysis of a particular case. In the second place, the distinction depends critically on how ascriptive, how fixed, membership of a class or of an ethnic group is. In this regard, Horowitz writes:

> (In Asia and Africa), (w)hat data on social class is available... suggests that social mobility is likely to mitigate the emotive component of class affiliations. (Case studies show that) a significant fraction of the urban poor manages to improve its material condition substantially... (T)he composition of modern-sector elites tends to be quite open to persons of various social backgrounds. This is largely due to the powerful influence of schooling in regulating access to elite positions and the tendency of secondary schools to draw students from a broad spectrum of the population. Given such patterns, it

comes as no surprise that interclass hostility is far (rarer) than is the desire for emulation of those of higher status:

(On the other hand), (e)thnic membership is generally given at birth. The ethnic group has a certain 'position' in society. Ethnicity and family are... connected. (These) ethnic affiliations have considerable power to generate conflict... (Horowitz 1985: 91,92)

There is then no analytic answer to the questions posed above. In societies (like modern South Africa) which have developed sophisticated urban-industrial economies, however, there is a distinct possibility that certain groups will have developed enduring class cultures, will have developed a shared status based on shared class position, and that - for such groups in given situations - these class cultures may play a more important role than those played by other communal affinities in the choice of an individual identity. This view is similar to that expressed by Crawford Young in his recent overview of scholarly works on modern Africa:

Ethnicity and class are autonomous determinants of social action; this must be conceded for any fruitful synthesis to occur... They differ in the forms of consciousness evoked, and the social idiom through which they are expressed. Ethnicity, an affective phenomenon by definition, is more readily mobilised... Class, because it is founded upon economic inequality, and embedded within the most influential contemporary political ideologies, may be a more deeply-rooted basis for conflict. Its activation requires assimilation into the social consciousness by metaphorical representations...
(Young 1986: 471,472)

Nationalism

An ethnic community shares many features usually attributed to a national community. Contemporary studies of nationalism[25] tend to emphasize the recent emergence of nations, their European heritage[26] and, accordingly, the contingent (rather than primordial) nature of modern nation-states:

Nationalism is a political programme, and in historic terms a fairly recent one. It holds that groups defined as 'nations' have the right to, and therefore ought to, form territorial states of the kind that have become standard since the French Revolution. Without this programme, realised or not, 'nationalism' is a meaningless term. (Hobsbawm: 23)

To Anthony Smith who is critical of too 'modernist' a view of this question:

Nationalism, through a modern and initially secular ideology, has breathed new life into ancient myths and old beliefs. It has strengthened existing myths of ethnic chosenness and kindled new ones wherever ethnic groups have begun to crystallize and demand recognition. We do not have to look to the consequences of industrialization, the inequalities of capitalism or the cold oppression of bureaucracy, not even to the hopes of democracy, important though these may often be, to explain why ethnic antagonisms are so intense and nationalist conflicts so frequent. Whether in Spain or Sri Lanka, the Horn of Africa or the Caucasus, the Baltic states or Kurdistan, the forms and intensity of these struggles derive in large part from the history of ethnic relations in each of these areas, and from the underlying patterns of ethnic survival and belief... (Smith 1992: 451)

Given this close affinity between ethnicity and nationalism, what manner of distinction should be drawn between them in the case of South Africa? Let us first note that a political programme launched by an ethnic group need not necessarily be a nationalist programme:

(T)here are vast areas of the globe, where ethnic politics, however embittered, are not nationalist, sometimes because the idea of an ethnically homogeneous population has been abandoned at some time in the past, or never existed... or because the programme of setting up separate territorial, ethnic-linguistic states is both irrelevant and impractical. (Hobsbawm: 24)

(E)thnie that have no intention of becoming nations, that regard themselves as ethnic 'fragments' in a wider *ethnie* the core of which lies elsewhere, even these must enter the political arena both for themselves and for the core to which they feel they are attached. By doing so, they hope to influence the policy of the state in which their fragment is incorporated, to pursue policies favourable to their ethnic core. Even if they have no core, they soon find that the competition of neighbouring *ethnie* within the same state requires a commensurate effort by themselves. (Smith 1986: 156)

The differences between the *claims* made by such ethnic groups and those made by nationalist groups are therefore relevant[27]. After listing six dimensions of an ethnic community - a collective name, a common myth of descent, a shared history, a distinctive shared culture, an association with a specific territory, and a sense of solidarity - Smith then points to two 'absences' from this list: 'One is economic unity, or a unified division of labour; the other common legal rights and a common polity'[28].

It is necessary, accordingly, to distinguish between nationalist claims, claims to sovereignty, to full territorial independence for the national community, and ethnic claims which are narrower, which are claims against government, and which are usually claims regarding resource allocation, such as employment opportunities in the common economy or in the state, or such as regarding land, or education and other welfare issues. Horowitz notes that '(j)ob-finding is one of the most important functions performed by ethnic associations throughout the developing world'[29].

When these group claims and group programmes become cast in a set of principles which form the basis for legitimising and mobilising group activities - when, in other words, the claims and programmes become elements of an *ideology* - then group identities tend to become more salient, group boundaries more clearly defined, and communities more integrated. This ideological dimension raises a fundamental issue:

> To say the modern world is a 'world of nations' is to describe both a reality and an aspiration. The legitimating principle of politics and state-making today is nationalism; no other principle commands mankind's allegiance. Even federations are always federations of nations. At the same time, few nations today are full 'nation-states' in the sense of being congruent and co-extensive. Not only are the ethnic populations of most states 'mixed', for most states have significant ethnic minorities and many are deeply divided; but the boundaries of these states do not often coincide with the extent of a single ethnic population. (Smith 1986: 129)

In so far as Smith's claim that nationalist ideology is as ubiquitous and pervasive as he states (and there are many who agree with him), then two consequences become clear. In the first place, ethnic claims and ethnic programmes - as defined above - will often incorporate strong emergent nationalistic tendencies, tendencies which seek sovereignty for the ethnic community[30]. Such tendencies may lead to changes in these ethnic claims and ethnic programmes, to changes which, at the limit, involve claims to control and dominate the state; or to demand secession, or partition, or irredentism ('a movement to retrieve ethnic kinsmen and their territory across borders')[31].

In the second place, the pervasiveness of nationalist ideology leads to movements which propose, and ideologies which seek to legitimate, 'nation-building' in plural societies, often - outside Europe and North America - conceived of on 'syncretic' lines, '(using) both European and non-European religions, beliefs, and symbols to mobilize people to demand democracy'[32]. Such 'nationalist' movements and ideologies have not fared well in the past. One quotation, written in 1986 with reference to Africa and which treats South

Africa as an exception, will suffice. The argument is well-known and generally accepted[33]:

> Beyond South Africa, nationalism as object of inquiry has gone into eclipse... The lack of staying power of post-colonial nationalist thought doubtless... relates to the relative absence of cultural content. In its most vital forms in other parts of the world, nationalism draws nourishment from the cultural resources that normally supply the inner core of the ideology... African culture as an ideological weapon was usable only in generalized, abstracted form, shorn of any ethnic specificity. The vocation of territorial unification embedded in anticolonial struggle denied to nationalism the emotive wellsprings which had supplied much of its energizing force in a number of other regions.
> (Young 1986: 436,437)

The development of terms such as 'ethnic nationalism' and 'ethnonationalism' reflect attempts by scholars to deal with the first consequence discussed above[34]. Likewise, the terms 'territorial nationalism' and 'African nationalism' are sometimes used to discuss the second consequence. These questions are clearly of direct relevance to modern South African society[35] and will be addressed below.

The study of ethnicity in modern South Africa

Our discussion has not addressed the 'vital essence' of the notion of ethnicity - a discussion which may well have become counter-productive[36] and have compounded the confusion[37]. It is widely accepted that ethnicity is Janus-faced, referring both to emancipation and to domination; to forward-looking claims and to backward-looking traditions; to constructed, invented and imagined communities and - at least to many members who identify with ethnic communities - to a primordial past. At the level of ethnic identity, numerous scholars argue that individuals choose, in different situations, from a range of possible identities. Ethnicity, accordingly, is situational, is episodic in appearance. It is also malleable[38]. Others argue that though this may well be the case, the sudden and dramatic emergence of an ethnic identity points to an underlying solidarity of a particularly communal and emotional kind, a solidarity similar to kinship and often based upon 'the deadly significance of symbols'[39].

How, then, should a discussion of ethnicity in contemporary South African society be approached? We have seen that race, in its second 'identity-related' sense, should be viewed as a possible form of ethnic identity and, therefore, as the basis of a consciousness which may lead to the establishment of an ethnic or racial community. We have seen that class position, particularly in modern South African society with its modern economy, may also lead to class identity and, accordingly, to community solidarity on the basis of a history of shared class position. In the third place, we have seen that many forms of ethnic consciousness include strong emergent nationalistic tendencies.

It would seem that we need to address, at the first level, the competition between these different possible identities in given situations and we need also to address, at the second level, the ways in which these given situations relate to the socio-economic, political and cultural histories of the communities within which individuals find themselves. And, in so doing, we need to bear in mind that 'ancient myths and old beliefs' and the 'existing myths of ethnic chosenness' very often are 'powerful, permeative, passionate, and pervasive' and should accordingly neither be overlooked, nor relegated to mere 'boundary markers' of other social, political and economic forces.

Finally, since these questions relate to individuals and communities in a plural society, it is essential to ask whether there are different emergent ethnic identities, and different emergent ethnic communities, within the same society. The focus of analysis cannot be solely on the society as a whole.

In one sense, the debate about the situational, constructed or primordial nature of ethnicity is an academic debate emerging from waning confidence in materialist forms of analysis, from the claim that 'we are all cultural hybrids' in the modern world, and from the inability of modern states to 'integrate' or 'assimilate' its citizens[40]. In another sense, it is a moral debate, a debate about universalistic and particularistic values, about human and cultural rights, and about how these rights should be upheld in contemporary modern states. It is appropriate, accordingly, to close this chapter by discussing the consequences, during the 1990s, of posing this ethnic question in South Africa society.

In the recent past, ethnicity has been widely viewed as an idea mobilised within the apartheid discourse of the South African government[41].

Neville Alexander, for instance, pointed to:
   the obvious and crude ways in which the present regime has 'moved away' from

racial terminology into ethnic terminology to effect the same purpose, justifying the disorganisation and exploitation of the working class. (Alexander 1985: 134)

Dubow, more recently, argued:
The notion of ethnicity has... been seized upon with alacrity by the government. (During) the late-*apartheid* era the concept has served as a convenient surrogate term for '*volk*' or 'race' - especially when international audiences are being appealed to. (Dubow 1993: 6)

In this form, it became, to Alexander, 'some kind of divine will or biological-cum-cultural fate'[42]. Desmond Tutu wrote, in 1984, 'We Blacks... execrate ethnicity with all our being'[43]. This misuse of the term - its use as a discourse strategy aimed at legitimating late-apartheid ideology - has tended to devalue and malign the term, the concept, and the questions which underpin it.

As a consequence, as I will show in detail below, scholars studying South Africa avoided or evaded these questions. For most, a serious discussion of ethnicity was perceived, incorrectly, to be tantamount to doing the apartheid government's intellectual work for it. The subject became a virtual taboo.

After the society entered its transitional phase in early 1990, however, events drove the question home. Ethnic questions, for reasons I will also show in detail below, forced themselves upon South African scholars. The troubled observations of two such scholars are illustrations:
Both personal experience and an increasing body of research show that ethnic identities have been widely accepted by significant numbers of Africans, and have at certain times, played a significant part in the manner in which South Africa has developed. In recent years moreover ethnic conflict has moved from remote rural areas, the alleyways in South African slums, and the inaccessible compounds, onto the streets and into the homes of the world in newspaper photographs and on the television screen. These pictures of ethnically-organised bands, their 'cultural weapons' in their hands, pursuing their enemies through the streets with horrifying results, is now a familiar image of South Africa in many parts of the world.
    For this reason, even those who believe that a discussion of ethnic divisions in South Africa gives the concept an unwarranted status and deflects the debate from the essential problem of the deeper forces which create and exploit ethnicity, cannot escape the fact that the violence in South Africa is being presented and widely accepted as 'tribal'. My own experience suggests that

these ethnic labels are gaining increasing currency. (Guy, 1992: 2,3)

Given the history of the word (ethnic) and its specific South African connotations, we clearly have to be very careful about the way in which we use the concept of ethnicity. This is not to advocate a doctrinal blindness to that which does not fit our theories or to explain away reality by means of scholarly niceties. Rather, it is to emphasize the necessity to bear constantly in mind that South African realities remain ideologically charged and that the impetus to locate South Africa in a comparative international sense - welcome as this is - should not obscure the particularities of its history. So long as we understand ethnicity as a malleable, historically conditioned process, and reject its use in categorical or reified terms which approximate to 'race' or 'population group', we may well be in a position to advance our understanding of this society's manifest complexities. (Dubow 1993: 17)

By 1993, then, some scholars are beginning to pick up the challenge. Adam and Moodley, reflecting a new pessimism regarding the 'new' South Africa, give serious consideration to 'a constitutionally entrenched right to secede under carefully regulated conditions and international arbitration'[44]. This work refers to the Zulu ethnic category. John Sharp and Emile Boonzaaier have recently completed a study of Nama ethnic identity which they describe as 'controlled performance'[45]. The study of ethnicity appears to be regaining a little credibility.

And, in a passage which is worth quoting at length, Joe Matthews, in provocative fashion, claims that a primordialist view of ethnicity exists on a wide scale in South Africa:

I am intrigued by the fact that the ANC, in its proposals on regions, managed to ensure that the dream of the Xhosas, to unite all the Xhosa traditional lands between the Fish River and the Umzimkulu River, will be realised. I know that everyone will say that this was not the intention. But it is an old dream; it's in the poetry; it's in the literature; it's been there for years. Everyone who has been taught Xhosa knows that that is a dream that started in the prophet Ntsikana's time.

The dominant Xhosa group doesn't accept ethnicity with regard to other groups. But when it came to their own area, they made sure that their goals would be realised...

I think this should be said, because if you discuss regionalism with the different groups it is unlikely that they will express their real wishes. Take, for example, my own people - the Batswana. We look at the various regional proposals and we see that the platinum mines have been placed outside the Tswana areas. And we say, now look here, we don't like this regional setup. We would like to make sure that all the minerals which have been under the control of the Tswana tribal groups and authorities since the last century should continue to be the financial base of any future region...

Similarly, we have very serious problems with those who belong to the former kingdom of KwaZulu, which was destroyed by the British. Many people have very strong feelings about restoring a united kingdom of KwaZulu, not necessarily in the form of a kingdom but certainly in the form of a federal state. And I don't think we should make the mistake that this is some kind of regional idea. Nobody can accuse the Zulus of having no ambitions to rule South Africa - if they can get away with it. That is what they would like to do. So we mustn't accuse them of being narrow regionalists in that sense...

It is no use treating the issue of the Afrikaners as if it is a mere matter of apartheid. It is not. It took half a million troops and support personnel to destroy the Afrikaner republics. Let's not think that that kind of situation can be brushed aside by a few words; by derogatory references to apartheid and so on. They believe in what they want. We must accommodate that; we must find a solution. (Matthews 1992: 26,27)

Nonetheless, alternative questions about South African society have dominated scholarly debates over the last fifteen years, and continue to dominate these debates at present. Mothlabi, for instance, writes:

At the root of the entire South African struggle and the main negotiation process is the conflict between the rightless majority and the privileged minority. (Mothlabi 1992: 54)

The next three chapters will show how these alternative questions were framed by scholars of modern South African society. They will also show why these rather than other questions predominated, and why - to most scholars - South African society was considered to be different from other societies.

NOTES

1. Most of the works listed in the 'International' bibliography apply, as do numerous in the bibliography on South Africa. It is of interest to note that Hobsbawm (1992: 24) argues that 'nationalism belongs with political science, ethnicity with sociology or social anthropology'. For a discussion of terminological and analytic confusion across academic disciplines, see Coulon 1990, Horowitz 1991b.
2. With regard to the two levels, see Roosens 1989, Smith 1992. With regard to questions relating to the first level, see Boucher et al. 1987, Martin 1993, Roosens 1989. With regard to stereotypes, see Horowitz 1985: 170,171.
3. Smith 1986: 22, Ch.2.
4. Smith 1992: 437.
5. Avruch 1992: 616.
6. Young 1986: 450.
7. Martin 1992: 326.
8. 'The event which served as the catalyst for the melding of diverse peoples into... a unit was the discovery of gold on the Witwatersrand in 1886.' (Vail 1989b: 7)
9. The definition of 'state' in international and South African scholarly works is a complex subject deserving separate treatment on its own (Bekker 1989). It is worth noting that, in Africa, the European model of the state has been widely 'imposed' (Martin 1992: 328). In this study, I will follow Degenaar by simply defining the state as 'comprising the triad of legislature, judiciary and executive which is responsible for setting the parameters of rule making in society and for the maintenance of order and justice through the enforcement of rules' (Degenaar 1993: 25).
10. Davis 1991: 16.
11. See, for example, Shaw 1986, Thompson 1989, Vail 1989a, Young 1986.
12. See, for example, Pieterse 1993, Vail 1989b.
13. As quoted in Murphree 1988:136.
14. Roosens 1989: 18.
15. Boonzaaier and Sharp 1988, Goldberg 1992.
16. Dubow 1987.
17. Thompson 1989: 1.
18. Horowitz 1985: 42.
19. Horowitz 1985: 22.
20. Horowitz 1985: 41f.
21. See, for example, Crawford Young 1986: 444, Hanf 1989: 89f, Roosens 1989: 15
22. I use Lipton's definition: 'By capitalism is meant a social system in which there is a substantial degree of private, as distinct from state or communal, ownership of the means of production (mines, farms, factories, banks)and in which the owners of these assets hire employees for a wage (or rent out their assets to others who do so) for private gain'. (Lipton 1985: 2).
23. Posel 1983: 60.
24. Smith 1992: 437).
25. See, for example, Anderson 1983, Gellner 1983, Hobsbawm 1992.
26. Noiriel 1991b.
27. Young 1986: 440.
28. Smith 1986: 31.
29. Horowitz 1985: 111.
30. Terminological confusion in the literature regarding the use of the terms 'nation' and 'ethnic group' is pervasive and deeply impairs comparative study (Horowitz 1991a) . In the modern South African case, as a result of widespread scholarly interest in Afrikaner nationalism - as will be discussed in the next chapter - it is essential to use clearly distinctive definitions of these two terms. The notion that the two ideas should be used in the same sense, or as different points on a continuum (see Legassick 1967, Southall 1985, Wolpe 1988, Yun 1990) may well have utility in modern Europe (Bratislava Symposium 1991), but leads to confusion and reductionism in the modern South African case.

31. Horowitz 1985: 281.
32. Martin 1992: 329.
33. See, for example, Doornbos 1991, Horowitz 1985, Martin
34. Yun 1990.
35. See, for example, Adam 1992, Alexander 1985, Giliomee and Schlemmer 1989a: Ch.12, Kane-Berman 1990b: Ch.3, Wolpe 1988.
36. Horowitz 1985: 55.
37. Glazer and Moynihan 1975: 1.
38. See, for example, Martin 1993, Pieterse 1993, Thompson 1989: 64.
39. Horowitz 1985: 57, 216.
40. On the notion of 'cultural hybrids', see Amselle 1990, Martin 1993. On difficulties of integration and assimilation, see, for example, Coulon 1990, Thompson 1989, Wunsch and Olowu 1990.
41. Posel 1987.
42. Alexander 1985: 137.
43. As quoted in Lijphart 1989: 14.
44. Adam and Moodley 1992: 510.
45. Sharp and Boonzaaier 1993: 1.

HOW UNIQUE IS SOUTH AFRICA?

A society which moved from rural Africa to urbanized and industrialized South Africa within three quarters of a century, if not less. (Maake 1992: 594)

Scholars have found it difficult to classify modern South African society together with societies of other countries. Historically, for example, this society has been compared to the American South and to societies of other Southern African countries. Its state has been represented as fascist and, often, as authoritarian. Sociologically, it has been to compared to Northern Ireland and Israel, and to countries in Latin America; and, in economic terms, to Taiwan and to the Republic of Korea[1]. A distinguished South Africa economist, in fact, claimed, in 1988, that 'South Africa, economically speaking, is only a generation away from becoming an advanced industrial society if historically achieved rates of growth can be sustained'[2].

It has traveled down neither the historical paths scholars have established for the British dominions, nor those for the ex-colonies of erstwhile European empires, nor those for the newly industrialised countries[3]. At least over the last fifteen years, it has been presented, typically, as different, as a special case.

A number of scholars went further by claiming that modern South Africa was 'unique', unique in the particular sense of manifesting types of political ideology and policy which are fundamental to an understanding of this society, and which are found nowhere else in the modern world[4]:

> In the end it is the unique adherence of the South African government to a policy of legally enforced racial segregation, employed to maintain the concentration of political and economic power in a small minority of the population, largely consisting of white persons of Afrikaner descent, which lies at the root of its failure to maintain the rule of law (Bindman 1988: 149).

> The South African state... differs from authoritarian governments elsewhere in fundamental respects that make it an illegitimate polity and an outcast among the nations of the world... Unlike any other country with ethnic conflict, South Africa imposes group membership from without... (I)t is the only country in the world that has legalized racial stratification.
> (Adam and Moodley 1986: 13, 15)

This tendency to claim a special kind of uniqueness has been identified and criticised by a number of international commentators[5]. Nonetheless, the particularities and complexities of modern South Africa, as they have been analysed in scholarly works, have also led to the observation that analysis itself of modern South African society has become a major problem for social science internationally. Consider the following recent assertion by a spokesperson of Unesco:

> The problem which South Africa poses to social scientists is not simply the condemnation of apartheid. There is the whole question of the explanatory efficacy of competing social science theories, for apartheid emerges both at the level of ideology and at the level of state organisation and policy - the racial allocation by the state of political, social and economic roles. Such racist practice is not an epiphenomenon in South Africa, neither is it simply the rationalisation of a form of advanced capitalism, nor is it only a form of settler colonialism. Again, it is not sufficient to say that South Africa is a racist society for race, although of central importance, operates there in specific ways and does not eliminate class formations. (Unesco Preface in Wolpe 1988: viii)

This 'international social science problem' is the subject of this chapter. I intend to show that modern South African society, through the use of frameworks of ideas, has been analysed on four basic axes, those of race, class, nationalism, and state. I will do this, first, by identifying the three dominant representations of this society developed by scholars. Subsequently, before attempting to define them, I will display them and point to their dominance by demonstrating the ways in which scholars subscribing to each representation have recognised and addressed claims and analyses made within the others. I will then argue that these representations have all addressed modern South African society and its history by using frameworks of ideas in which race, class, nationalism, and state are central. Although there is some variation in the conceptualisation of these ideas, and fundamental differences in their theoretical primacy, they form the critical scaffold of ideas for each of these scholarly representations.

My subject, accordingly, comprises the manners in which scholars have attempted to understand 'modern South African society'. In this respect, it is both important and remarkable to note that the essence of these scholarly endeavours is to understand the society as a whole, its state and the territory under that state's jurisdiction, that state's definition of races, the emergence of economic classes within that state's territory, and the nature of the nationalism which claims control over that state. Whether this essence refers to 'the common society', the 'social formation', or the 'republic', the general assumption exists that an understanding of life in modern South Africa needs to be, or at least needs always to refer directly to, representations at the macro-level, at the societal level. This scholarly assumption seems to imply that being a modern South African stamps one with a unique, albeit differential, 'South-African-ness', in contradistinction to other inhabitants of the planet.

A scholarly representation is based on empirical research, and claims both to analyse a particular society comprehensively, and to elucidate its history. It is underpinned, moreover, by an identifiable methodology as well as a general framework of ideas and, at least in the case of the three at issue here, each contests the validity and utility of other scholarly representations. Of most importance to this work, a representation is a system of ideas which is both constructed by, and, once crystallised, which directs, scholars in their work. It follows that a scholarly representation is not fixed, and always needs to be identified, during a given period, as an ideal type. The fact that it is an ideal type, not always capturing the nuances and elaborations within the body of work defining it, is inevitable in an analysis of this nature, but I intend to show that there are three dominant - intellectually influential - representations of modern South African society which have recently been created and elaborated by scholars.

Since this definition is crucial to my argument, let me be clear about what my claim comprises. The works on modern South African society under consideration here been produced by a community of scholars. This community has developed certain scholarly norms which are applied when work undertaken within the community is evaluated. Though neither fixed nor uncontested, these norms are used in cross-references, some critical and some approving, to such works. Such references signal relevance to the manner in which South African society is being analysed. The presentation of empirical evidence - to validate argument and explanation - is one of the most important mutually accepted norms. Since the community of scholars - in the case of the body of scholarly work relevant to modern South African society - is an international one, the subject of this chapter is accordingly directly related to the international social science problem alluded to above.

Before addressing these representations, one more point needs to be made about their identification. Since scientific objectivity in the study of modern society is not possible, it is clear that all such representations will include normative and forward-looking elements, and, accordingly, may develop ideological tendencies. It is the empirical analysis and justifications for this analysis which are at issue in a scholarly representation, not the ideological elements of the representation itself, present (or emergent) though they may well be.

Intellectual works which propose - as their main purpose - a future 'African nationalist', or 'nonracial', or 'broad South African nationalist' society, for instance, important though they may well be as objects for scholarly analysis, are ideological works rather than empirical analyses of modern South African society. This is so since scholars have not identified these works as defining methodologies and historical and contemporary analyses of South African society which differ from those of one of the three dominant scholarly representations[6]. I have, accordingly, not considered them as belonging to bodies of work which define scholarly representations.

On the other hand, where it is clear that scholarly works have been used for both representational (empirical-analytic), and ideological or political purposes, I have attempted to select the more 'scholarly' or 'academic' versions as my sources[7].

The three dominant scholarly representations of modern South African society

In the recent past, three dominant representations of modern South African society have been developed by scholars. I will call the three representations the *liberal*, the *marxist*, and the *Afrikaner nationalist* representations.

During the last fifteen years, different opinions regarding the salience, and hence the influence, of these representations in scholarly circles have been expressed. One such opinion is that the challenge for scholarly supremacy has been won by the marxist representation. In a 1991 study proposing a normative study of South African society, Atkinson, a liberal scholar, wrote that:
> (b)y the 1970s, the prevailing 'liberal'... approach to South African political analysis was decisively dethroned by a materialist paradigm. This new perspective has set the tone for various subsequent approaches to political analysis. (Atkinson 1991: 59)

She then pointed to the 'state-centric' theory (which emphasizes the role of the state in political matters), and the 'ideology-critique' theory (which pays close attention to language subjectivity and thought) developed by scholars working within this representation.

She continued by arguing that these scholars:

> are methodological realists... According to this spirit of enquiry, everyday symbols and interpretations conceal 'true', or more fundamental, forces or structures... marxism exercised particularly great influence on the work of (these scholars, for whom) the dynamics of the state and the content of ideologies were largely determined by powerful class forces. Economic classes, not race ideology, was the motor of history, and classes were structured according to the relation of the members of society to the means of production.
>
> Having delineated social reality into relatively superficial structures and more fundamental ones, (these scholars) then argued that the former was functional to the maintenance of the latter. In the context of South African history, it was argued that racial discrimination was functional to the development of capitalist exploitation... Whereas liberals saw capitalism as a beneficial modernising force, (these scholars) regarded it as a class exploitative system. (Atkinson 1991: 61-67)

Alexander, a marxist scholar and activist, while addressing members of the Association for Sociology in Southern Africa in 1984, addressed the question of scholarly supremacy in the following manner:

> Even today, more than ten years after the university-based radical assault on the liberal approach to the study of Southern Africa began, almost every new contribution has to submit to the tortuous necessity of debunking the myths of liberalism...
>
> (W)e have won the battle against the liberal approach to the study of society. (I)t has become much more urgent for us to alter our conception of our tasks by becoming, in Gramsci's phrase, 'organic intellectuals' whose functions are firmly based on the interests of the working class - in South Africa, the black working class! (Alexander 1985: 128)

On the other hand, in 1988, Simkins, a leading liberal scholar, had the following to say 'about the much-discussed relationship between race and class in South Africa':

> Mocking class-based analyses of South Africa, the English sociologist Frank Parkin once observed that applying class analysis to what is so obviously a racial system is about as appropriate as applying functionalist integrationalist analysis theory to the modern Lebanon. In fact, (I do) not rely on such extreme

a view. For much of South Africa's history, the development of economic classes has taken place without straining the racial estate system. But economic development has now reached the point where the further evolution of class relations cross-cuts and undermines the racial estate system.
(Simkins 1988: 134)

Some years earlier, in an article pleading for a less reductionist and functionalist marxist approach to race and class in South Africa, Posel had this to say about the liberal representation:

(T)he liberal understanding of the economic underpinnings of South Africa's political system is confined within a methodologically individualistic problematic; that is, the economic determinants of racial policy are characterised in terms of the intentions and volition of particular individuals and groups thereof. Class forces, on this view, represent merely the arithmetic sum of the power of influence of such groups... However sophisticated an interpretation we give of the liberal position, it still stops short of an understanding of the role of objective class forces which both constrain and enable individual intentions and actions, and which are not fully subject to conscious individual and group control. (Posel 1983: 60,61)

Simkins, in the same work quoted above, claimed that an 'individualist' approach, based on Rawlsian principles, does not 'prevent (a scholar) from considering any analysis of an actually existing society, including analysis of classes and power':

For nationalists... the essential category is the group and not the individual. Some nationalists would speak of the 'group subject', just as some marxists would speak of the 'class subject'; both, by so doing, contrast their standpoint with those that concentrate on the 'individual subject'... (The) apparently stark opposition between the individual and the group as subject can be reduced by working from both ends. Liberalism is not committed to the view that human units are self-contained and as like any other as one atom of a given element is like any other atom of that element (though) this is sometimes used as a simplifying assumption in economic analysis... (B)eing a member of some community and engaging in many forms of co-operation is a condition of human life and introduces the concept of a social union... Or, to put the matter another way, human sociability need not - indeed ought not - to be left out of account by liberals. (Simkins 1988: 131, 149)

There are numerous other influential liberal criticisms of the marxist representation, and marxist criticisms of the liberal representation[8]. Suffice it to say that though the liberal representation has remained one of the dominant representations during the period under discussion, its scholars have been driven, increasingly, to address in their works claims made within the emerging marxist representation. Before turning to the Afrikaner nationalist representation, it is illuminating to illustrate this debate by considering the works of historians subscribing to the liberal and marxist representations.

In its often quoted 1969 preface, the liberal editors of *The Oxford History of South Africa* proposed the following approach to South African history:

This work derives from our belief that the central theme of South African history is interaction between peoples of diverse origins, languages, technologies, ideologies, and social systems, meeting on South African soil.

It is peculiarly difficult to write the history of a society as rigidly stratified as South African society. Recent histories of South Africa illustrate the difficulties. Nearly every one of them embodies the point of view of only one community. The group focus is seen in the structures of the works as well as in the interpretations they give to events...

The reasons for these limitations are evident. Group focus is the product of the social milieu in a plural society, where communication between the different communities is restricted and the individual historian is conditioned by the assumptions and prejudices of his own community, whether it is a community of religion, or class, or language, or race, or some combination of two or more of these factors...

(G)roup focus is a product of social division and becomes less conspicuous as a society becomes more homogeneous. (Wilson and Thompson: 31,32)

By 1978, Davenport - one of South Africa's foremost liberal historians - had this to say about 'the current debate' in South African scholarship:

South Africa's isolation arose from social policies which came to offend not only black South Africans but the independent African states, the communist world, and the liberal democratic states of the West. The government's commitment to these internationally unpopular policies - a commitment endorsed by the plebiscite of half a dozen general elections since 1948 - has elicited various kinds of explanations. These tend to fall into two main groups: explanations which see racism as the chief determinant of white South African attitudes, and explanations which attributed them to a clash of class interests...

(The former explanation assumes that) (e)conomic rationality urges the polity forward beyond its ideology... (the latter explanation that) the apartheid system was designed primarily to assist the capitalist mode of production under South African conditions rather than to protect the interests of the white(s)...

At bottom, the debate... was over the possibility of evolutionary change. (Davenport 1978: 370f)

By the late 1980s, prominent historians had recast the history of twentieth century South Africa within the marxist representation. I have selected as illustrations two short passages from a book entitled *The Politics of Race, Class and Nationalism in Twentieth Century South Africa:*

> As the South African economy recovered from the depression and the pace of industrialisation quickened, thousands of recently proletarianised workers made their way to the towns from the impoverished white farms and the increasingly desolate reserves. Appalling living conditions, low wages and inadequate transport coupled with the brutalities of the South African state fueled the dramatic urban protest movements, the growing trade-union organisation and the sporadic strikes of these years (the 1930s and 1940s). (Marks and Trapido 1987: 47)

> Large factories, new technology and the total inability of the Bantustans to subsidise welfare costs transformed the position of the black working class during (the 1970s). The early 1970s saw a formidable growth in African working class militancy, with 98 000 workers involved in strikes in 1973; this was followed by the Soweto uprising of 1976, the culmination of seven years of African regrouping and student activism... (Marks and Trapido 1987: 54)

Chapters in this book then analysed the 'changing ideological strategies of the state, capitalists and the parliamentary opposition' for which '(t)hese economic changes and political developments form the background'[9].

Justification for the selection of the Afrikaner nationalist representation as a dominant one is more complex. In the first place, as a nationalist movement, it was judged by its scholars to have realised its major mission when, in 1961, the Republic of South Africa came into being. In the words of an Afrikaner nationalist historian:

> (An) important facet of South African history during the years 1948-1961 is the victory of Afrikaner nationalism over its old enemy, British imperialism. Whereas the Afrikaner had previously been dominated by British imperialism, since 1948 he has not only succeeded in freeing himself completely from its toils, but also mastered his opponent. Afrikanerdom has now disposed of all signs of its past degradations... There was one dream... which had still, however, not been realised: a Republic of South Africa... (It) came into being on 31 May, 1961. (Liebenberg, B.J. in Muller, C.F.J. (ed.) *500 Years: A History of South Africa* 1969: 392-394)

The result of this national victory was Afrikaner nationalist control of the South African state, control which led to the elaboration of apartheid ideology and practice. In a study which refers, *inter alia*, to the works of such international scholars as J A Hobson, Hans Kohn, and Henri Pirenne, a leading Afrikaner nationalist academic philosopher and historian argued as follows:

> The Afrikaner subscribes to a republican state and to a parliamentary system of government. He believes that the people of South Africa should rule themselves without foreign intervention. He believes that each nation (*nasie*) should rule itself; he rejects political integration (i.e. a unitary state) in favour of political differentiation (singular (*eiesoortig*) and separate development). Until such a dispensation is established in South Africa, the Afrikaner together with other worthy Whites must retain the power of the state. These are the principles of Afrikaner nationalism. (Kotzé 1968: 54. My translation.)

The domination which such a view necessarily involved - temporary domination of one nation over others, as perceived and recognised within the Afrikaner nationalist representation - had two consequences for this representation. The first was dissension, either for ethical or for political reasons, among influential Afrikaner nationalist intellectuals. In the words of Hermann Giliomee, an Afrikaner scholar who has broken from the Afrikaner nationalist representation:

> From the late 1960s, Afrikaner unity began to crumble... Various intellectuals who had originally helped to formulate the apartheid ideology started to break away from the NP for very different reasons... For instance, N.J.J. Olivier, who broke away to join a liberal party to the left of the NP, was representative of the group of Afrikaner nationalists who propagated a 'liberal nationalism'... Olivier found it impossible to condone the fact that apartheid had become a cloak for massive discrimination and injustice. In contrast, others such as Albert Hertzog and Andries Treurnicht, who formed conservative parties to the right of the NP, were staunch nationalists and would not approve of the watering down of apartheid. Both pledged that they would restore the Calvinist principles and work for the viability of the *volk*. (Giliomee and Schlemmer 1989b: 59)

The second was the growing incorporation into this representation of the apartheid ideology. Giliomee put this case as follows:

> A nationalist movement rarely has clear and coherent ideas about the most desirable political and social order. It is through its association with another, more specific ideology (socialism or fascism, or, in the case of the Afrikaner nationalists, apartheid) that it acquires an action-related system of ideas... (Over the past forty years), there was, on the one hand, the Afrikaner nationalist ideology with its claim to the land and Afrikaner sovereignty in that land. Apartheid, on the other hand, was an operative ideology that spelled out the relations between whites and other ethnic groups (or 'nations') in South Africa in a way that both fostered and concealed Afrikaner rule. (Giliomee and Schlemmer 1989b: 41)

What then became of the Afrikaner nationalist representation during the period under consideration? In the first place, it became, particularly to Afrikaner scholars who have broken from it, an object, a cultural, intellectual and historical object of inquiry in itself[10]. Through a deconstruction of this representation, by proposing through empirical research that its historians, for example, have become 'captive to the nationalist paradigm', to use Andre du Toit's phrase[11], these studies have established significant new dimensions to the representation of modern South African society, dimensions which were absent from the liberal and marxist representations. Giliomee's analysis cited above is one example. It is useful to illustrate the novelty of this approach by way of another example, also drawn from work by Giliomee.

In an analysis which proposes that conflict in modern South African society is 'essentially... between two communities, predominantly Afrikaner and African respectively, whose primary aim is control of the state and possession of a historical homeland', Giliomee assembled empirical evidence to argue that:

> (Though) recent analyses of Afrikaner nationalism concentrate on economistic explanations, and in some cases virtually exclude the political and emotional dimension... (this) dimension - issues relating to communal power and status - is crucial, and indeed decisive... Ultimately, (Afrikaner nationalism) goes beyond culture, and involves a close emotional attachment with the State, national institutions such as Parliament and the army, and national symbols and values. Much of the talk about a peaceful transition of power in South Africa misses the fundamental point: that the Afrikaners and the larger white nation consider their sovereignty as precious. It is not something to be bartered away. (Giliomee and Schlemmer 1989a :118-121)

In the second place, intellectuals loyal to the representation took on the burden of attempting, both ethically and in the interests of conserving that paradigm, to marry its dominant Afrikaner nationalist nature to its parallel apartheid ideological element. Consider first the troubled analysis of a leading Afrikaner nationalist sociologist, in a study of modern Afrikaner attitudes to race relations in South Africa executed in the mid-eighties:

> An important implication of Afrikaner ethnicity for intergroup attitudes is that the politicisation of this ethnicity - and hence Afrikaner nationalism - will prevail as long as Afrikaner ethnicity remains the primary basis for the dominant constitutional position which the Afrikaner occupies in the South African dispensation... When due consideration is given to the inevitable competition over the power of the South African state, it is justified to infer that

Afrikaner ethnicity and Afrikaner nationalism are essentially complementary. And if we agree with Banton's scholarly claim that 'there has been only one nationalism in South Africa, that of the Afrikaners', we must then heed another reality, namely that the vast majority of non-Whites probably consider ethnicity to be of minor importance. In other words, important though Afrikaner ethnicity may well be as a basis for democratic reform in South Africa, the fact that the Coloured population, for example, clearly rejects Coloured ethnicity is of equal importance. (Rhoodie and Couper 1986: 110-112. My translation.)

In sharp distinction is the political and ideological discourse (concealing Afrikaner nationalism, if Giliomee is correct) employed by an Afrikaner nationalist professor of political science who subsequently became Deputy Minister of Information and of Constitutional Affairs in the South African government. During a 1988 academic conference on the problems and prospects for political accord in the country, he proposed, and offers justifications for, seven principles underpinning that government's 'framework for the future'. The seventh principle, 'private enterprise', represents an important shift toward universalistic values in the ideology. The principles are:
> (A deviation from majority rule) to accommodate the cultural and historical peculiarities of (South Africa);
> the principle that no single group should be able to dominate other groups or the entire political system;
> peace and stability... not only in the future political system, but also in the process leading up to (it);
> political or constitutional reform cannot develop in isolation, (but need) to be accompanied and underscored by development and reform on the social and economic fronts;
> the principle of decentralisation of decision-making, as far as possible;
> the maintaining of Christian values and civilised norms; (and)
> an economy based on the protection of private enterprise.
> (van der Merwe 1989: Ch.4)

In the third place, the Afrikaner nationalist representation has been re-established by a new social and political movement in the country, the white right-wing, with the Conservative Party as its political torch-bearer. '(This) movement is fundamentally Afrikaner nationalist in orientation. Its ideal is the creation of an Afrikaner-dominated nation-state in which Afrikaner values and culture may flourish in safety and security, a state in which the principle of Afrikaner self-determination may unequivocally be applied by Afrikaners, and unambiguously recognised by other people'[12].

The intellectual roots of this movement are found in earlier Afrikaner nationalist thought; its intellectuals are still found in some South African universities; and its representation of modern South African society differs from the earlier representation in only one major respect: the fact that the Republic of South Africa, in its present territorial form, has not realised the Afrikaner nationalist mission[13]. Consider the following 1987 analysis by C J Jooste in an article entitled *'n Land vir die Afrikaner*, published in the (once) prestigious Afrikaner nationalist *Journal of Racial Affairs*:

> From his very beginnings, the Afrikaner has attempted to share his land with foreigners for whom assimilation is not possible. Foreign nations (*volke*), or many members of such nations, have been attracted by, or been allowed to enter, the economic sphere.

The consequence, Jooste argued, is the present 'cul de sac' (*doodloopstraat*) in which Afrikanerdom finds itself. To find a way out, to establish a new Afrikaner nation-state (*volkstaat*), requires that the following conditions be met:

> Granting the principle of the alienation of land with a view to effective partition and nation-building.
>
> No use is served by alienating more land than can be occupied and defended by the nation, or by that part of the nation which will live there. This will merely result in a repetition of the history of foreign incursion (*indringing*) and foreign threats.
>
> The exclusion of foreign workers should take place fairly (i) by ensuring that all land and resources in the new (Afrikaner) state will be exploited, (ii) by so implementing partition that similar viable territories may be established for other nations, and (iii) that appropriate development aid is made available to neighbouring states. (Jooste, as quoted in Grobbelaar, 1991: 326, 327. My translation.)

In a recent analysis of a scholarly work by Andries Treurnicht (the main leader of this new Afrikaner nationalist movement until his death in 1993), Schutte argued:

> Unmistakably, Treurnicht considers the (Afrikaner) nation (*volk*)... the determining sphere of life. He considers the individual to be subject to that community. Race, language and culture are considered to be the basis for a nation. Sovereignty in one's own circle represents national independence. (Schutte 1987: 403)

Fragmented though it undoubtedly has been into deconstructed, apartheid-ideological, and narrower re-established elements, the Afrikaner nationalist representation nonetheless is recognised as dominant in the works of other scholars. As a new cultural object of enquiry for Afrikaner scholars, as has been shown, it has led to significant innovative dimensions in the scholarly representations of South African society. To some marxist scholars, it has posed perplexing questions. Isabel Hofmeyr, who used a materialist approach to analyse 'the manufacture of an Afrikaans literary culture' in the early twentieth century, concluded her study as follows:

> (The) contradictory and unstable process (of being made into an Afrikaner) lies at the very heart of nationalist ideologies during the first two decades of this century. Furthermore, in locating the genesis of nationalist thinking in (such an) unstable process, one can hopefully resuscitate some of its complexities which have for far too long been muffled under the deadening weight of organic and idealist interpretations. These analyses tend to reduce nationalisms to inert categories of language and religion which somehow suggest themselves from below. This object of this chapter, however, has been to show that these relationships are perhaps less predictable and more arbitrary than traditional wisdom has lead us to believe. (Hofmeyr 1987: 116)

While addressing modern Afrikaner nationalism and Afrikaner nationalist identity, Adam and Moodley admitted similar puzzlement:

> What makes people accept one or other explanation of reality remains one of the most vexing questions in the social sciences. The marxist answer 'class interests' is shown to be inadequate when people in the same class adopt conflicting ideologies. Whatever makes equally wealthy farmers in the Transvaal, or teachers in the Free State who have identical material interests, nevertheless define their political stances so differently escapes economic reductionism. (Adam and Moodley 1986: 64)

Though it has - as a result of fragmentation and loss of coherence - lost influence in established scholarly circles, the Afrikaner nationalist representation remains important, by challenging common wisdoms within the other two representations, and by way of a narrower process of renewal.

Liberalism, marxism and Afrikaner nationalism

The *liberal* representation, as we have seen, proposes methodological individualism as its approach to the study of South African society. Empirically, individuals acting in different ways at different times are the focus of analysis and, ethically, classical Western constitutional 'freedoms of the person, of speech, movement, association and equality before the law' ought to apply to these individuals[14].

When faced with a modern plural society, in which 'peoples of diverse origins, languages, technologies, ideologies, and social systems, meet', liberal scholars developed a number of principal themes rooted in this methodology. Under which conditions would these 'diverse peoples' interact freely as individuals? Which institutions promote such interaction? And which institutions inhibit such interaction?

The analyses which resulted from such questions flow from three widely-held liberal views of modern South African society. In the first place, the process of modernisation is believed to be the great 'individualiser', implying, in the words of Simkins, 'democratisation both in the form of popular participation in government and in the widespread enrichment of life chances'[15]. The now classical 'O'Dowd' thesis of South Africa's stages of economic growth is an apt, and much criticised, example[16]. In 1990, Kane-Berman identified the following eight elements of what he called South Africa's silent revolution: 'urbanisation', 'education', more and more blacks in... skilled jobs', 'changes in income distribution', black consumer spending', 'African home ownership', and' the rise of the informal sector'[17].

In the second place, a powerful image of an ideal liberal society - 'the common society'[18] - informed liberal scholars. This image is based largely on works of (English) philosophers and (American) social scientists belonging to the school of political pluralism[19]. 'According to this conception, society should be seen as including a series of intermediate and relatively autonomous institutions: trade-unions, churches, political parties, and not just in terms of the 'state' and individual members. These institutions mediate between the people and the state... guarantee the individual freedom of association, and counter the formation of potentially divisive groups'[20]. References to such an ideal liberal society are explicit in the recent work of Simkins[21]. It is noteworthy that neither classes in their marxist sense (which would undoubtedly become 'divisive') nor nations (which would claim control over the state) are included in this ideal society. What is included in this image is a 'process of socio-economic liberalisation'[22], a process which leads, in a capitalist society, to 'the widespread enrichment of life chances'.

Given these two conceptions of South African society - the actual unequal plural conception and the future ideal pluralist conception - a major concern of liberal scholars became how to move from the one to the other, how the one may evolve from the other. Hence, the continuing search for a negotiated settlement, for a peaceful method of transition[23]. Hence also, the need to address socio-economic issues during this period of political transition. Writing before February 1990, Kane-Berman argued: 'The real issue, now, is how the backlogs in black amenities would be eliminated. This is a far greater challenge to South Africa than merely repealing the remnants of discriminatory legislation'[24].

In the third place, the more liberal analyses of modern South African society revealed that the modernisation path - economic development notwithstanding - was not 'individualising' South Africans, not leading toward a pluralist democracy, the more these scholars sought explanations in the racial structures and state policies of the time. In 1973, 'South Africa's political system is a racial oligarchy in which all significant political power is vested in white hands'[25]. In 1979, '(t)he uniqueness of South Africa as a racially divided society lies in the extent to which its historically determined lines of conflict have been hardened and reinforced by statutory measures'[26]. And in 1988, 'South Africans are the prisoners of traditions which limit the scope of strategic manoeuvre, (and of) cross-pressure, special interest groups'[27].

There is, in fact, a consistent image in liberal South African thought of the unfree individual, enduring an imposed racial identity, imprisoned in unequal racial compartments, captive of nationalist and racist traditions, garrisoned by an all-powerful Afrikaner nationalist state, by a laager state under siege. Two issues are crucial in this image: the statutory racial divide supporting race stratification, and the all-powerful state which succeeds, against the currents of economic development and modernisation, in preserving this system of race stratification.

Before turning to a similar definition of the marxist representation, let us note the ways in which 'race' and 'state', two fundamental ideas of the liberal representation, are used within this representation. It is the imposed nature of racial identities and of the racial divide, thereby precluding individual freedom and interaction, which is at issue. This idea of race uses the term in its 'official' and imposed sense as an outcome, rather than as a 'formation', rather than as a construct in the minds of different South Africans[28]. Within the liberal representation, increasingly during recent analyses, race is addressed structurally.

With regard to the state, it is the concentration and centralisation of power, thereby precluding the development of cross-cutting, intermediate, relatively autonomous institutions, which is at issue. This view of the monopoly of power by the state leads to the need to address modern South African society holistically, to address the question of 'the common society'. Within the liberal representation, analysis moved to the macro-level.

The *marxist* representation, as we have also seen, proposes methodological realism as its approach to the study of South African society. Empirically, it is 'objective class forces' which are 'the motor of history' and these classes are 'structured according to the relation of the members of the society to the means of production'. '(T)he indispensable starting point of an analysis of contemporary South African society is the process of capital accumulation and correspondingly the relations between capital and labour'[29]. Ethically, conflict between these classes ought to result in national liberation and a socialist society[30].

When faced with the 'social formation' of modern South Africa in which the 'emergent black working class is characterised by 'appalling living conditions, low wages and inadequate transport coupled with the brutalities of the South African state', and the capitalist class is characterised by 'rapid monopolisation of capitalist production... leading to the emergence of a more united, dominant, monopoly group'[31] marxist scholars developed a number of principal themes rooted in this methodology.

In the first place, this approach identified class interests as fundamental. Accordingly, as shown in the (often quoted) passage below, a number of key questions were identified:

> Who owns what? Who does what? Who gets what? Who does what to whom? Who does what for whom? How are who does what and who gets what linked to who owns what and who controls what? How is all this linked to what is going on in society and history?
> (Johnstone as quoted in Atkinson 1991: 67)

In modern capitalist South Africa, this led to three broad themes. In the first place, there were analyses of capitalist consciousness, capitalist action and capitalist strategy, in particular with regard to the convergence of capitalist and state interests. The marxist view of the relationship between capital and the state in a capitalist society is a functional view: the state represents (or ought to represent) capitalist interests, and therefore legitimates (or ought to legitimate) these interests through its ideology. In the second place, there were analyses of emergent worker consciousness, worker action, and worker strategy. Thirdly, there were analyses of worker struggles against capitalism and against the state, analyses which simultaneously sought for socialist elements in these struggles.

The marxist representation includes an implicit theory of change. The earlier South African social formation comprised a mix of capitalist and pre-capitalist modes of production. As capitalism and white domination developed (through reproducing themselves), and as the Black working class strengthened and confronted their opponents, identifiable crises took place. These crises define periods and conjunctures in South Africa's capitalist development[32]. The class struggle inherent in these developments leads to a revolutionary struggle. There is 'no middle road'.

There is accordingly a powerful revolutionary idiom in the marxist representation. Given two conceptions of South African society - the actual unequal capitalist and white domination conception and the future ideal (classless) socialist conception - change from one to other takes place through a serious of phases, during which capitalism and the struggle against capitalism 'mature', as it were. This process culminates in fundamental change, change of the mode of production, by way of a revolutionary struggle. One classical path - as conceptualised by viewing the Russian, Chinese and Cuban revolutions as intellectual exports - is the socialist route. Since, however, the French Revolution is a competing intellectual export, marxist scholars have focused particularly on the distinction and relationship between national (in the French revolutionary sense), and socialist, liberation and revolution.

The more marxist analyses showed that modern South Africa had not reached its socialist revolutionary phase, the more sophisticated their principal themes became.

Structures (such as class consciousness, or the state and its ideology) which were expected - theoretically - to be more superficial and hence functional to more fundamental structures (such as capital and the working class itself) were treated as having more autonomy, as being more 'contingent'[33].

Accordingly, analyses of the persistent racial divide within classes led to questions regarding the White, the Afrikaner, and the Black working class, and regarding their respective bourgeoisies.

Analyses of the differing actions and strategies both among, and between, capitalists and state organisations led to questions regarding capitalist interests underpinning state policies (such as separate development); regarding the importance of cleavages, 'fractions', within the capitalist class; and regarding the differing forms of capitalist legitimation - the different ideologies - employed by this class.

In the third place, there were analyses of the strategies and actions of the trade-union and liberation movements which were perceived to be gaining strength during the phase coinciding with the period under scrutiny in this study, as well as analyses of their main political opponent, the militarising state. Marxist scholars identified closely with the Black trade union and liberation movements, and sought to identify, and promote, the socialist elements in these movements' ideologies and strategies.

The consistent image in scholarly marxist thought on modern South Africa is that of a conflictual capitalist society. It is this social formation, established by a capitalist economy in a settler colonial society, which fashions the incompatible interests of capitalist and worker, largely of White and Black. The Afrikaner nationalist apartheid state came to be the guardian of this social formation, and thereby the enemy of the Black working class. South Africans are unfree in the sense that Black communities are dependent upon this social formation, the working class is exploited by the capitalist system, and members of the White bourgeoisie are moulded by their material interests, by the drive to monopolise profit, by the greed, inherent in the social formation. It is through continual confrontation, struggle, and crisis that fundamental change comes about, that a socialist society may emerge. The development of South African capitalism transforms South Africans into class members who then oppose one another as classes on an intensifying scale until the revolutionary socialist struggle frees them all from capitalism.

Before turning to a similar definition of the Afrikaner nationalist representation, let us note the ways in which 'class', 'race' and 'state', three fundamental ideas of the marxist representation, are used within this representation. First, 'class' is used in a realist sense. In a capitalist society, it is the relationship of individuals to the means of production that is primary.

Unless individuals are class-conscious, their 'real' class interests remain concealed. Class is an objective concept.

With regard to 'race' and 'state', earlier comments made regarding the liberal scholarly representation remain valid. In realist marxist analysis, 'race' is viewed structurally, as imposed by the state, as supportive of capitalist interests, and, therefore, as inimical to working class interests. Race is viewed as an ideological 'outcome' rather than as a subjective construct.

The 'state', perceived to be acting as the guardian and defender of capitalist interests of an increasingly monopolistic kind, seeks itself to monopolise political power throughout the society. Marxists scholars need, accordingly, to address modern South African society holistically, to address this 'social formation' at the macro-level.

The *Afrikaner nationalist* representation proposed methodological holism as its approach to study South African society. This approach was idealist and cultural-sociological. It was also fundamentally primordialist. This primordialism is found in the conception that an individual could only find real expression through his or her nation. Hence, an individual could only become a complete human being through loyalty to this nation, through speaking its given language, through conforming to its given traditions, and through devotion to its given religious creeds.

The major issues addressed within this representation were Afrikaner issues: Who are we Afrikaners? Where are we going? What is the point of our existence as a people, and what has happened to us as a people?[34] Its ethical orientation was toward the achievement of political sovereignty for the Afrikaner people, a national mission underpinned by a particular Christian theology based on Calvinist ideas. Its theory of change was rooted in the organic mobilisation of this people in a struggle for republican independence. For other peoples living within the plural society of South Africa, equivalent opportunities for nation-state formation were envisaged.

In contradistinction to the two other dominant scholarly representations, the Afrikaner nationalist representation lacked an explicit theory of economic development. Since its approach was idealist and organic, the influence of materialist forces on national consciousness was perceived to be secondary. Thus, though separate nations in separate territories were conceived of as developing separate economies, there was no adequate empirically-based theory underpinning this conception.

Other than that individuals, in particular Afrikaners, become free insofar as they are able to express themselves as Afrikaner nationalists in an Afrikaner nation-state, there is no consistent image - during the last fifteen years - in scholarly Afrikaner nationalist thought on modern South African society. Earlier thought conceptualised the Afrikaners as a small beleaguered nation, colonised by the British and surrounded by alien forces and influences, a nation which could defend itself solely though communal solidarity. It was through participation in Afrikaner social, cultural, moral and economic life, and through the assimilation of Afrikaner nationalist history, that this solidarity, and ultimately national loyalty, was to be sustained. And it was through political mobilisation that the mission of Afrikaner nationalism - the quest for an Afrikaner republic - could be realised.

As the apartheid state controlled by Afrikaner nationalists entrenched its political authority, during a period of rapid economic development, Afrikaner nationalist thought developed and elaborated elements of authoritarianism and of state-imposed racism, and of the protection of social and economic as well as cultural features of the Afrikaner community. Increasingly, Afrikaner nationalism and its 'operative ideology' of apartheid merged, and developed into an integrated system of legitimatory ideas. Domination over other South Africans - particularly African South Africans - emerged as an increasingly important element of this integrated ideology. Nationalist aims gave way to apartheid practices, and, hence, justification for such aims needed to be replaced by justifications for such practices. These are sufficient reasons to understand the Afrikaner nationalist scholarly dissension and fragmentation we identified above.

Still-life South African identities

One way to draw together the different strands of these scholarly representations of modern South Africa is to ask in which ways they have addressed *the identities of individual South Africans*. I have accordingly developed an account of what these scholars understand a South African to be. The account I shall give is 'frozen'. It does not address the theories of change scholars have proposed within their representations. It is therefore more properly a caricature, rather than an analysis or summary. The purpose of the caricature is two-fold: to underline the importance of the notions of race, class, nationalism, and the state in these scholars' thought; and to illustrate the focus scholars have maintained on 'South Africa as a whole'.

How have scholars of modern South African society visualized the identity of a modern South African? In still-life colours, the answer is relatively simple:

A modern South African is either Black or White.

A Black South African is either African, Coloured, or Indian. A Black South African is probably a poor worker, employed or unemployed. If he or she is not a worker, this Black South African is probably an even poorer African South African living in a rural area of a homeland, or in an urban informal settlement. Since these peripheral areas are deeply affected by the modern urban-industrial South African economy, this African South African hopes to become a worker. The chances are slight that a Black South African is a capitalist, and are extremely slight that an African South African is a capitalist.

The South African state has compartmentalised all Black South Africans in this way. Accordingly, to some scholars, a Black South African views himself or herself either as Black (or as becoming Black), or as African (or as becoming African). To other scholars, a Black South African views himself or herself as a worker (or as becoming a worker).

A White South African is different. A White South African is either Afrikaans or not Afrikaans.

An Afrikaner South African is probably a nationalist. An Afrikaner nationalist South African strives for an independent Afrikaner nation-state. Because there are more Afrikaner White South Africans than White South Africans who are not Afrikaans, the South African state is controlled by the Afrikaner South African. He or she has become rich through this control. Because there are fewer White South Africans than Black South Africans, an Afrikaner South African uses the state to compartmentalise all South Africans into separate homelands. An Afrikaner nationalist South African hopes that these homelands will become separate nation-states.

A White South African who is not Afrikaans is probably a capitalist. Therefore, a White South African who is not Afrikaans is richer than an Afrikaner South

African. Accordingly, to some scholars, a capitalist South African disagrees with an Afrikaner Nationalist South African over state control since this may harm capitalism. To other scholars, a capitalist South African agrees with an Afrikaner Nationalist South African over state control since this may benefit capitalism. The chances are slight that an Afrikaner South African is a worker and very slight that a White South African who is not Afrikaans is a worker.

Accordingly, to some scholars, a White South African who is not Afrikaans views himself or herself as a capitalist (or as becoming a capitalist), whilst an Afrikaner South African views himself or herself as a nationalist (or as remaining a nationalist). To other scholars, a capitalist South African and an Afrikaner nationalist South African both view themselves as White (or as becoming White).

Each South African, according to these views, exhibits a primary identity and plays a primary role in his or her society. It is the nature of the society as a whole, dominated by the central apartheid state, that is the context within which this takes place. It is the primacy of imposed racial classification, of class divisions, and of Afrikaner nationalism that defines these identities, and prescribes these roles.

In this sense, modern South Africa has been presented as unique, as a society where, economic development notwithstanding, individual identities are more imposed, more separate, and more given, than in other societies. And the causes for this imposition, for this separation, and for this ascription are to be found, scholars have argued, in the political economy of the society. Each South African's identity and each South African's consciousness emerges from this political economy (rather than from language, or from communal culture, or from religion, or from region, or from heritage...).

NOTES

1. See Frederickson 1981, Vail 1989a, Simson 1980, Greenberg 1980, van den Berghe 1990, Gann and Duignan 1991.
2. Simkins 1988: 1.
3. Berger and Godsell 1988.
4. See, for example, Slabbert and Welsh 1979: 11, Thompson in Thompson and Butler 1975 : xv and those quoted below.
5. See, for example, Berger in Berger and Godsell 1988: 267, Horowitz 1991a: 27, Lijphart 1989: 16.
6. It has been asserted that 'Africans made two kinds of responses to capitalist development in modern South Africa. The first expressed adherence to the 'ideal of a racially integrated South Africa... as exemplified in the development of the African National Congress... The second tendency has been the obverse of the first... The Pan-Africanist Congress... was representative of this (latter response)' (Lodge, as quoted in Stadler 1987: 142). These responses have regularly been analysed within scholarly works as images of South African society and as ideologies which African leaders (and other Africans) constructed for themselves. Rarely, if ever, were such images transformed into new scholarly representations by these leaders themselves. I will offer reasons for this absence in Chapter V.
7. I have selected, for instance, Slabbert and Welsh 1979 rather than PFP policy documents, Wolpe 1988 rather than SACP policy documents, and van der Merwe 1989 rather than South African government policy documents.
8. See, for example, Adam and Moodley 1986: Ch 1, Slabbert and Welsh 1979: Ch.2, Stadler, Wilson 1975, Wolpe 1988: Chs 2 & 3.
9. Marks and Trapido 1987: 55.
10. See, for example, du Toit 1984, 1985, Giliomee in Giliomee and Schlemmer 1989a, 1989b, Schutte 1987, and Slabbert 1975.
11. du Toit 1984.
12. Grobbelaar et al.1989: 44.
13. See, for example, Grobbelaar et al. 1989, Grobbelaar 1991, van Rooyen 1991.
14. Sprocas 1973: 17.
15. Simkins 1988: 1.
16. See, for example, Davenport 1978 : Ch 20, Leftwich 1974, Lipton 1985
17. Kane-Berman 1990b: Ch.1.
18. See, for example, Macmillan 1991.
19. See Degenaar 1977.
20. Bekker 1977: 34.
21. Simkins 1988: 64,73.
22. Kane-Berman 1990a: 371.
23. See, for example, Sprocas 1973 , Slabbert and Welsh 1978, Simkins 1988, Schlemmer and Giliomee 1989a, 1989b, Kane-Berman 1990.
24. Kane-Berman 1990a: 371.
25. Sprocas 1973: 21.
26. Slabbert and Welsh 1979: 11.
27. Simkins 1988: 18.
28. I owe this formulation to Adam Kuper, Conference on Ethnicity, Identity and Nationalism, Rhodes University, Grahamstown, April 1993.
29. Wolpe 1988: 14.
30. Wolpe 1988: Ch.2.
31. Hackland 1987: 383.
32. See, for example, Saul 1988, Wolpe 1988: Chs 4 and 5.
33. See, for example, Posel 1983, Wolpe 1988.
34. See, for example, Moodie 1974, Schutte 1987.

SCHOLARSHIP IN ISOLATION

*Where else but in relation to South Africa can moral totalitarianism be presented as an **academic** virtue.* (Tom Young, as quoted in Cohen *et al.* 1990: 16 Emphasis in the original)

The scholarly representations and theories upon which debates regarding the nature of South African society stand, are largely home-grown. It is striking to note the extent to which virtually all recent influential analyses are based upon South African scholarship. This is clearly reflected in the bibliography included in this work. Recent South African history and historiography have been developed by South African historians. In sociology, anthropology and political science, works by South African scholars predominate; in the legal field likewise[1]. This body of indigenous scholarly knowledge - in comparison to many countries in Africa, Asia or Latin America, for instance - is probably exceptionally large. Indeed, it may be said that South African scholarship, albeit at a cost as will be shown below, has succeeded in freeing itself from its earlier British imperial dependence. The disciplines of history and anthropology are apt examples.

As has been shown, these scholarly representations and theories have been highly contested within the scholarly community. Over the last fifteen years, liberal scholars have been consistently and sometimes fundamentally challenged by growing and increasingly sophisticated marxist scholarship. Afrikaner nationalist scholarship, though clearly in decline, with many of its scholars questioning establishment orthodoxy, or breaking from the 'laager', remained a significant third alternative, albeit increasingly marginalised. In effect, there has been no agreement among South African scholars about the basic features which make up modern South African society[2] about 'the burden of the present', as an American historian once called it[3]. The result, as Stone put it, was to be 'locked into a particular political or intellectual position... the fate of so many scholars writing about South African society'[4].

Foreign scholarly influence took on two forms. In the first place, a number of South African scholars left the country - often in the sense of seeking exile - and continued to analyse South African society at academic and research institutions in other countries. England, the United States, and Canada have been the three main 'receiving areas'. These scholars and their institutions acted as important scholarly centres, simultaneously introducing new ideas and acting as sounding boards for developing South African scholarship. Most worked within the marxist representation, others - typically at different institutions - within the liberal representation. Internal scholarly dissension, accordingly, was exported[5].

In the second place, a number of foreign scholars[6] selected South African society as an object of enquiry. They usually collaborated closely with selected groups of South African scholars and tended to elaborate on existing representations and theories developed within South Africa. There were, of course, some exceptions, analyses which introduced new ideas and approaches specific to South Africa. Contributions by Elphick in history, by Meillassoux in history and anthropology, by Berger, Hanf and Johnstone in sociology, and by Gann and Duignan, Huntingdon, and Lijphart in political science are some examples. In particular, there were highly stimulating comparative studies drawing on knowledge largely unknown to South African scholars. Examples of such studies are those of Frederickson in history and Greenberg in sociology[7]. Most of these works have tended to have a differential effect in the scholarly community within South Africa, being assimilated into one of the dominant representations whilst being criticised and subsequently rejected by others.

In short, it would appear that the dominant representation of South African society today is both *highly contested* by different scholarly traditions each of which has strong mutually reinforcing influences, and *largely indigenous*, domestically produced by scholars who were born, and have lived and worked, in the society.

There are two sets of reasons for this: the first, a scholarly environment increasingly isolated, both from the outside world and, domestically, within the society itself; the second, a domestic scholarly environment within which scholars accomplished their work with deep commitment and conviction, often accompanied by a sense of moral outrage.

Domestically, these scholars were faced with a government increasingly ostracised internationally and with the major South African movements of political opposition in exile. They were also faced with a widening strategy of international embargo (including an academic boycott), and with a policy, in effect, of non-collaboration by international development agencies. Accordingly, the South African scholarly community found itself increasingly isolated, deeply divided within itself, and largely alone. Thus, representations of contemporary South African society (as well as scholarly proposals for 'post-apartheid' South Africa) rest in large measure on ideas and theories developed by South African scholars on the basis of their differing South African experiences. Comparative experience was difficult to acquire (since travel, for South African passport holders, to most Third World countries was prohibited), and comparative knowledge often viewed as esoteric or irrelevant (since South African society was typically viewed as 'unique').

This image of South African scholarship does not imply that most of their ideas and theories are superficial, of little use, or deeply flawed. To the contrary. Most South African scholars have benefited from extensive material support from their institutions and from high esteem for their vocations. A number of these institutions have consistently struggled to defend the rights of scholars to study and publish their works in an intellectual environment free from ideological and other state-imposed constraints. Accordingly, a number of South African universities[8] and non-government organisations[9] (NGOs) have developed sophisticated research cultures within which major dimensions of South African society and the challenges facing this society have been addressed. A large and often advanced body of basic and applied knowledge regarding these issues has developed.

What this image does carry within itself is the notion of a scholarly environment which is not only intellectually but also socially and culturally isolated. While assimilating and applying in their work the new international ideas and norms spreading around the globe of human equality, of non-racialism, of emancipation, and of individualism, these scholars were confronted daily with a society - with *their* society - which systematically and fundamentally rejected these ideas and norms, which compartmentalised South Africans into separate and evidently unequal categories. Scholarly work became, therefore, much more than simply a cerebral task. It implied constantly applying the values and principles used during this work, within the society to which they, together with their families, colleagues and friends, belonged. In such an environment, accordingly, many scholars developed a zeal, a determined political commitment, and a deep sense of moral outrage about the nature of their society.

This isolation and its concomitant 'hot-house' effect on the scholarly community does not mean that the representations and theories developed by members of this community are without a European heritage. To the contrary, the core ideas employed to analyse South African society, namely, race, class, nationalism and state are all of European origin.

Justifications for this claim have already been given in Chapter IV. The claim is not that the theories and ideas are European in the sense of being direct intellectual imports. It is clear that they have been tested and moulded with regard to the histories and activities of South Africans[10]. The claim is that they would not have achieved the primacy they did in the scholarly representations we have identified, had they not had European roots.

The idea of race, and its related ideology of racism, were imported and elaborated by Europeans who settled in South Africa. Conceptions of class, likewise, were largely elaborated by European intellectuals, particularly after the Russian Revolution of 1917. Afrikaner nationalism has deep roots in European and particularly French revolutionary and Dutch ideas of national emancipation[11]. Analyses of the South African state owe much to Weberian and more contemporary European conceptions. South African scholarship, in this sense, may be seen as a European fragment[12], currently isolated from, or confined within narrow corridors of, new and innovative thought elsewhere.

This conception of scholarly thought as a European fragment may be transferred to the South African community of scholars. It is largely empirically correct to view this community itself as an isolated European fragment. Though mainly South African born and bred, these scholars have been overwhelmingly White, and most have belonged to an international anglophone culture. The Afrikaner minority has been drawn increasingly into this international culture. Few Black South African scholars, and very few Africans, have belonged to this community. There have, of course, been exceptions. For example, Nolutshungu in England; Biko, Manganyi, Mphahlele, Ngubane, Ramphele and Zulu are, or were, prominent African scholars[13]. Nonetheless, as a result of sustained discrimination and exclusion over a long period of time, Black scholars have had little opportunity to develop skills and to find positions with which they were able to compete with their White compatriots.

This highly skewed constitution of the South African scholarly community has recently been described by a number of Black South African scholars. In a work bearing the subtitle *Insider Accounts of Apartheid*, the editors wrote:

> The accounts provided in this book make something of a break with the intellectual traditions of South African scholarship in history and the social sciences. The authors represented here reflect the coming of age of a new and vigorous strand of scholarship, drawn from the small ranks of black intellectuals, professionals, and social scientists. In the past this group has been intellectually marginalized by the hegemonic position and numerical dominance of white scholars in the old 'liberal' universities... or prematurely dismissed because they were forced to work in institutions created by the apartheid planners. (Cohen *et al.* 1990: 1).

There are, therefore, more than intellectual reasons - as analysed in Chapter IV - which may be given to explain the scholarly claim that modern South Africa is unique.

Most scholars were South African and White. Increasingly drawn to international ideas and norms which they considered to be in direct conflict with those imposed by the South African state, these scholars conceived of their society as fundamentally different from others, particularly from those (which they knew best) that did apply these international ideas and norms of equality and of non-racialism. Since these scholars lived materially privileged lives in a highly unequal society, moreover, they were constantly kept aware of the consequences of apartheid ideology and practice on the Black (and particularly, African) majority of their compatriots. Their concerns were consistently pitched at the societal level where what they considered to be fundamentally different and warped principles and practices were identified and analysed.

The community of scholars was deeply divided. Part of the reason for this division is to be found in differing assumptions about human and social behaviour, particularly regarding the role of self-interest in motivating behaviour. Simultaneously, the divisions signaled different political commitments which related directly to potential change in South African society as a whole. As Merle Lipton put it with regard to 'The Debate about South Africa':

> (T)he issues are bitterly contested... because this debate... is an integral part of the political struggle over the future of the country from which many of the aspiring future leaders have been exiled; and these issues, apart from their theoretical and scholarly interest, have important implications for policy and strategy towards SA. (Lipton 1985: 12)

This community was also increasingly isolated. As a result, knowledge about different circumstances in other societies, particularly societies outside the north-eastern quadrant of the globe, was limited. Comparisons intended to reveal features shared by both South Africa and certain of these societies were rarely made. As a result, corruption and nepotism in South African homelands, for example, tended to be explained comprehensively as direct consequences of South African government policy and manipulation, whereas comparisons to other societies may well have elaborated and qualified such explanations[14].

Isolation also led to a pervasive emphasis on South African society on its own. The campaign of international sanctions strengthened this view. The object of enquiry became a 'state isolate', a unique society rejected by the international community and yet succeeding in retaining autonomy through central state repression. Writing in 1977, R W Johnson observed:

> In most of the enormous literature on South Africa there is a strong tendency, in which left-wing radicals and Afrikaner nationalists are at one, to depict South Africa's development as if it were dictated solely by the internal dynamics of her own history. This assumption is false at least for the whole period since white settlement in South Africa began in 1652. (Johnson 1977: 15,16)

In short, for social, cultural, moral and intellectual reasons, South African scholars experienced their society as 'particularly' unique, and thereby developed a notion of 'South African-ness', a particular quality that was experienced differently by different South Africans, which set members of modern South African society apart from other inhabitants of the planet. Although there was a small group of dissidents, foreign scholars of modern South African society tended to reinforce this view.

NOTES

1. See, for example, Boulle 1984, Mathews 1990, and extended references in Bindman 1988
2. Horowitz 1991a: Ch. 1.
3. Wright 1977.
4. Stone 1992: 635.
5. London, Oxford, York and Warwick in England, and Yale University in the USA are examples.
6. Some scholars are difficult to classify. For instance, I do not consider Heribert Adam who has spent long periods of time at South African universities, as a foreign scholar.
7. See the bibliography for references to such works.
8. The open liberal universities are examples, and, more recently, the Universities of Durban-Westville and the Western Cape, together with a number of Afrikaans-medium formerly volks-universities.

9. The South African Institute of Race Relations, the Urban Foundation, as well as a number of church organisations may serve as illustrations.
10. With regard to the Dutch roots of Afrikaner nationalism, Schutte has commented as follows: 'The birth of the Afrikaner people and their national consciousness... are of course the product of South African history and the developments within South Africa itself. Consequently, research into the origins and development of Afrikaner nationalism that is limited to the history of abstract ideas will never produce a satisfactory overall picture.'
11. See, for example, du Toit 1985, Schutte 1987.
12. Harz 1964.
13. See the bibliography for references to such works.
14. For examples of such explanations by South African scholars, see Cobbett and Cohen 1988, Vail 1989a: Ch 14. For explanations of similar occurrences elsewhere, see Klitgaard 1988, 1991.

RECENT STUDIES ON ETHNICITY IN SOUTH AFRICA

Reluctant though one may be to admit it, the presence within a single society of large racially and culturally distinct groups is an almost certain source of at least some measure of social strife and disorder.
(A. S. Mathews 1990: 66)

The claim made in the introduction that 'there is little discussion on ethnicity in South Africa at the moment' is not meant to imply that scholars - during the last fifteen years - have not analysed phenomena which they considered to be 'ethnic'. Rather, the claim is that these phenomena and the ways in which they were treated by scholars led to a common wisdom that ethnicity was either unimportant, or epiphenomenal, or dependent upon more 'fundamental', upon 'deeper', forces in modern South African society. As we have seen in the previous chapters, these forces were conceived to have arisen from structures and ideologies fashioned by race, class, nationalism and the state, from structures and ideologies at the societal level.

The purpose of this chapter is to analyse a carefully selected body of scholarly work which has addressed 'ethnicity' in South African society. The need for selection is self-evident: the scholarly literature is enormous.

The selection will be guided by two criteria. In the first place, the scholarly works selected need to have been written during the last fifteen years. In the second place, by virtue of the theories and questions which a number of academic disciplines and scholarly representations have developed, I have selected those in which one may - for methodological and theoretical reasons - expect 'ethnicity' to become an important issue. In this regard, I have also selected three broad disciplinary approaches: sociology and political science, history, and anthropology. Needless to say, I claim that such an approach is neither exhaustive nor comprehensive. Nonetheless, these carefully selected illustrations are intended to show that this widespread common wisdom had developed in scholarly circles by the early 1990s.

That there are always a few exceptions is one of the great gifts of free empirically-based academic discourse. In the case under discussion in this chapter, there are two types of exceptions. There are a small number of scholars who argued against the common wisdom, who did consider ethnicity to be a major issue in South African society. Their scholarly works will be noted and discussed. Simultaneously, a large body of work relating to ethnicity among (White) Afrikaners has been written[1]. In the previous chapter, it was argued that one important consequence of the fragmentation of the Afrikaner nationalist representation in the early seventies was the definition of the history and evolution of this representation as an historical and cultural object of scholarly inquiry. As a result, *Afrikaner* ethnicity and its relationship to Afrikaner nationalism became a major scholarly issue. Though reference to these works will be made, they do not form the main focus of this chapter.

The first body of work selected is that produced by sociologists and political scientists who adhere to the liberal scholarly representation. Since individual identities, attitudes and prejudices - in particular, those of a political nature - are primary to these scholars, one would expect the issue of ethnic identity to become primary in a modernising society represented as 'the interaction between peoples of diverse origins, languages, technologies, ideologies, and social systems, meeting on South African soil'. I shall also refer to Afrikaner nationalist scholars in this section since the same issue should also have been of direct concern to them during the late apartheid period of South Africa history.

If we expect this first group of scholars, by virtue of their methodology and theories, to pay particular attention to individual identities, we should expect historians to have addressed the question of the existence and histories of 'cultural communities' in South Africa. In the 1980s, this has been done by a group of marxist historians, and their work, accordingly, has also been selected.

In the third place, we have seen that each of the three dominant scholarly representations have led scholars to address modern South African society at the macro-level. This resulted in a general disregard for sub-societal, potentially ethnic, processes of community formation and communal mobilisation. These were only perceived to be relevant insofar as they related directly to processes at the state level. Race, in its imposed structural sense, and class were seen to be the great divides. Since it is one of the major purposes of anthropologists to study human interaction at the micro- rather than at the macro-level, one would expect their work, together with that mentioned above, to have addressed ethnicity seriously. This body of work, therefore, represents the third and final selection.

Sociology, political science and ethnic identity

An analysis of recent scholarly works in these disciplines must begin with the identification of the idea of 'the plural society'. This idea was widely used and was deeply influential[2] during the 1960s and 1970s. Its use with reference to South African society came under increasing criticism[3] during the latter decade and its influence, accordingly, waned dramatically, except in Afrikaner nationalist scholarly circles.

The idea of a plural society, originally developed by Furnivall and elaborated by M G Smith and others, points to the coexistence of culturally different groups, lacking shared values, within a colonial society. Members of these different groups meet in the common market place, the common economy, as individuals. In the absence of legitimacy, the colonial state keeps the society together through coercion.

M G Smith emphasized cultural pluralism, arguing that cultural institutions within the different groups making up the plural society were incompatible one with the other, and, accordingly, that conflict inherent in such societies was largely due to these culturally and socially incompatible institutions.

Criticisms of such analyses of South African society emphasized a number of deficient elements in this scholarly representation. It proposed an essentially static, ahistorical, model of this society. Hence, cultural groups - 'ethnic communities' - tended to be treated as fixed, as primordial, and barely able to change as the society changed. The inadequacy of this assumption led some pluralist scholars to conceptualise, in classical liberal fashion, processes of individuation inherent in the modernising economy of South Africa[4]. In short, the development of a modern urban-industrial economy and its effects on the plural nature of the society, it was argued, could not be analysed adequately within this representation. Simultaneously, this assumption led to the co-optation, by apartheid ideologues, both of the term 'plural', and of certain arguments originally made by plural society scholars[5].

The plural society representation was also criticized for not recognising the changing political conditions, and the rise of modernising elites from different categories, within modern South African society. Accordingly, the view emerged that the conflict potential inherent in South African society should not be located mainly - if at all - in the incompatibility of cultural groups, but in the political struggles between representative groups of minorities and majorities, of the privileged and the excluded. In short, the changing role of the apartheid state, and of opposition to that state, it was likewise argued, could not be analysed adequately in this way.

The demise of the plural society representation led to two important shifts in liberal (sociological and political) thought among scholars of South African society. The first was a deeper and more consistent focus on socio-economic[6] issues, on inequality, poverty, and their social consequences within the society as a whole. This was coupled with a parallel focus on socio-political[7] issues, on government apartheid policies, on their territorial, racial, and economic consequences, and on possible paths for evolutionary democratic change. In the second place, a focus on cultural issues - on issues regarding the changing values of different categories in South African society - faded rapidly.

It is this fading of scholarly interest in cultural, in ethnic, issues that is our focus in this section. I will first address works which fall broadly within the discipline of sociology, and subsequently address those more aptly described as belonging to political science.

The sociologists

In 1975, Michael Savage wrote:
> The more industrialization has drawn ethnic groups in South Africa together - geographically, economically, *culturally* - the more White rulers have attempted to impose their distinctions between ethnic groups and maintain a social distance between them. (Savage 1975: 284. My emphasis.)

By the late 1980s, as illustrated in a book of collected essays entitled *Critical Choices for South Africa: an agenda for the 1990s*[8], the only reference to ethnicity (in the sense I have defined above) is reflected in the quotation (from A S Mathews) given at the beginning of this chapter. This quotation is of interest because it recognises the highly sensitive nature - verging on a taboo - of academic discourse on ethnicity in modern South Africa. This problem will be discussed in the next chapter.

Other than this brief reference to ethnicity, the 'critical choices' in the large majority of chapters are defined as socio-political and socio-economic, not of a cultural nature[9]. Major cleavages in modern South African society are identified along socio-economic, socio-political, and imposed racial lines. The major issues comprise change of the minority white government and its apartheid policies, of centralised state organisations, as well as changes in growth and redistribution within the South African economy.

Such brief references to the existence of ethnic identities in modern South African society have become common-place. An example from a liberal review of race discrimination in South Africa[10] will be given. In a chapter describing the imposed and discriminatory systems of education which operate in the society, Auerbach commented in passing as follows:

> Undoubtedly, African educators in South Africa, if they had a free hand in drawing up syllabuses, would wish to include aspects of, for example, precolonial African history, and interpretations of the history of African tribes in South Africa which are not now being taught... (Auerbach and Welsh: 81)

In other sociological chapters in the review, ethnic identities or ethnic consciousness are not addressed at all.

The fading of scholarly interest in cultural, in ethnic, issues is even more striking in the case of recent analyses of conflict in modern South Africa. Consider the manner in which two prestigious members of the scholarly community, Andre du Toit and John Kane-Berman, approached the question of conflict in the Natal region during the late 1980s. Two major incidents of inter-ethnic conflict took place in 1985 in this region, and a process of violent conflict in the Natal Midlands and in the Durban area (which resulted in at least 1500 deaths) persisted during 1987 and 1988[11]. An analysis of each of these conflicts could include, at least as an important hypothesis, the issue of symbolic and political struggles over who legitimately claimed to represent the 'Zulu' (as well as more generally accepted issues relating to material inequalities).

In a remarkable work on political violence in South Africa, du Toit proposed discourses on political violence as a method of getting to grips with the dilemma regarding under which conditions political violence may become legitimate. His analysis hinged on the rejection of the state as the pole around which such legitimation should revolve. In the same work, the Natal Midlands conflict is discussed[12], and described (though not analysed) as 'a civil war in which the forces of tradition and conservatism seem ranged against the young'[13]. Neither in the lengthy introduction to this work (co-authored by du Toit), nor in du Toit's chapter were (possible or partial) ethnic bases for this or other conflict in the Natal Region violence analysed[14]. The framework of analysis was political, oriented toward state action and toward opposition to the state, and the imposed racial divide was fundamental to the analysis.

In another remarkable work identifying the crumbling of apartheid in South Africa, the Midlands and Durban conflict was described in terms of 'rivalry' between 'the two organisations', the ANC and Inkatha[15]. Reference to ethnicity or to ethnic conflicts is found nowhere in the entire work. The framework of analysis was socio-economic and socio-political, and the imposed racial divide was fundamental to the analysis.

The imposed racial categories compartmentalising South Africans into four 'population groups' became the fundamental categories within which liberal sociologists located their analyses. Not only were official statistics presented in this form, but attitudinal and resource surveys relied on them as the basis for studies of differing interests, identities and life chances[16]. Development studies in South Africa followed a similar route, ignoring the potential importance of ethnic identities and ethnic communities in development programmes[17].

One of South Africa's foremost liberal sociologists, Lawrence Schlemmer, has been more careful in this regard. Influenced by work done by Theo Hanf (1981) in the early eighties, he has consistently pointed to potential ethnic conflicts in modern South Africa. In 1980, in a work based upon wide-ranging survey data in different parts of the country, he wrote:

> Because South Africa is a divided society... a painful part of reform is the adaptation of identity politics... Unifying symbols (of national unity, identity reassurance and goal definition) will not emerge very easily. Race and ethnicity, and the frustration and relative deprivation which both amplify, will constantly threaten to abort the good effects of reform and leave only the heightened expectations that reform brings. (Schlemmer *et al.* 1980: 38)

In 1989, he argued as follows:

> Ethnic identities do exist among the African majority. Seen very broadly, there is evidence that such identities have social and political consequences... These results notwithstanding, in a situation in which all ethnic categories among Africans feel more or less united in protest against the common factors of their exclusion from Parliament, it is easy to find evidence supporting inter-ethnic political unity at the grassroots level.
> (Giliomee and Schlemmer 1989b: 167,169)

Finally, in a paper addressing violence in the South Africa of the 1990s, he stated:

> Ethnic identity is what one may term a 'floating' phenomenon... Therefore, it is incorrect to see antagonistic ethnicity as an inevitable *prior* factor (to violence). It is perhaps more often than not a consequence. Once activated, however, it focuses hostility on 'out groups' very sharply, can be deadly in its effects, and does not abate for a long time. It would be naïve not to expect ethnicity (in South Africa) to become activated in the current conflict. It is going to make the violence immeasurably more difficult to deal with. (Schlemmer, 1991: 9,10. Emphasis in the original)

It is important to note that Schlemmer only addressed the first level in our conceptualisation of ethnicity, that of ethnic identity. Without a thorough analysis of the second level, that of ethnic community and its history, the emergence of ethnicity seems to take on a mysterious quality, becoming 'a floating phenomenon', as Schlemmer puts it. Nonetheless, the importance of the phenomenon was clearly recognised.

This recognition was absent in many undergraduate curricula offered by South African universities. In the late 1980s, the Department of Sociology at the University of South Africa - a department catering to the largest number of under-graduate sociology students in the country - did not offer a course (and did not address academic literature) which focused on ethnicity as an issue. Nor, in 1990, did the Department of Sociology at the University of the Witwatersrand, one of the most prestigious in the country[18].

Though not the focus of analysis in this section, it is of interest to identify the primary ways in which marxist sociologists approached the subject. Loyal to their scholarly representation, ethnicity was perceived to be constructed in the interests of a class. I have selected works by Gerhard Maré to illustrate both the difference in approach, and the fact that the study of ethnicity - particularly in the late 1970s and the 1980s - was not considered important.

In 1987:

> What happened in South Africa... clearly illustrates a process in which 'cultural pluralism' becomes the politicization of tribal differences... In other words, pre-capitalist social, economic, and political forms of organization are artificially maintained or recreated. However, they are in distorted form, and in a context where they have very little real relevance (other than to create antagonisms and to serve as a handy point of reference if conflict should arise). (Maré and Hamilton: 31)

In 1992, in a work which addressed ethnicity in a significantly more serious fashion, Maré nonetheless argued that:

> Ethnic groups... do not exist outside of social identity... There is no *structured* position in society that determines an individual's membership of an ethnic group, in the way that economic relations determine class membership. An ethnic group may, or may not, exist. The fundamental relationship in society remains, therefore, a class relationship, without claiming an essential course of action associated with membership of a class. (Maré 1992: 40 Emphasis in the original)

Two surveys by South African scholars of the international literature on ethnicity, facilitated by extended visits to the USA and Western Europe to assemble recent international literature and opinion, were completed during the early 1980s. I have classified the two scholars, G S Cloete (1981) and Nic Rhoodie (1985), as conforming to the Afrikaner nationalist representation. Cloete's work culminated in a constitutional proposal for South Africa. After completion of this work, he became - in the mid-eighties - a senior member of a South African state department responsible for constitutional issues and was subsequently summarily dismissed from this position together with a senior colleague. During the 1960s and 1970s, Rhoodie had been a loyal, though critical, Afrikaner nationalist scholar.

Cloete's concern was constitutional and legal. Accordingly, his definition of ethnicity[19] tended toward the primordialist view and his comparative analysis of constitutional arrangements in other countries also tended to 'freeze' ethnic communities into legal and constitutional categories. This tendency is, in a sense, a necessary and potentially dangerous consequence of any search for constitutional arrangements which explicitly address ethnic communities. Yash Ghai, an international constitutional lawyer, for instance, argues that ethnicity changes over time, thereby creating the need constantly to renegotiate state strategies based upon ethnic group membership[20].

Rhoodie's work was more directly sociological. It distinguished between identity, political and socio-cultural dimensions of ethnicity, included a broad and well-argued survey of much of the international literature, and concluded with an analysis of the importance of ethnicity and nationalism in modern South African society. The conclusion drawn from this analysis was similar to that he made a year later[21], a conclusion discussed in Chapter IV above.

It is probably not fortuitous that the only two comprehensive surveys of this nature (that I know of) which were undertaken in the 1980s, had both been written in Afrikaans and completed within the (apartheid-ideological) Afrikaner nationalist representation. The subject was of critical interest to the ideologues of the apartheid state, and of deep sensitivity to liberal and marxist scholars.

In the mid-eighties, the Pretoria-based Human Science Research Council completed an investigation into inter-group relations in South Africa. Drawing on a wide range of liberal and Afrikaner nationalist scholarship, it published a report which proposed 'a scientifically accountable description and explanation of the nature and processes of intergroup relations in South Africa'[22]. Though ignoring most marxist scholarship on the society, this courageous attempt by a state research body to question government orthodoxy addressed ethnicity in South Africa in a deeply ambivalent fashion:

> ... South Africa is a multi-ethnic country in which ethnicity under the Afrikaans-speaking white is accommodated by the policy of formal group institutions, but... some other groups do not wish to be accommodated on this basis at present. In this sense the question as to whether the plural community of South Africa is *mainly* an ethnic pluralism, must be answered in the negative. The group delimitations in South Africa are therefore not simple, nor are they necessarily intrinsic to groups. (HSRC 1985: 63. Italics in the original)

In conclusion, bearing these few exceptions in mind, scholarly sociological attention to cultural and ethnic phenomena in modern South African society had waned substantially during this period.

The political scientists

Liberal political scientists, in the 1960s and 1970s, were faced with a 'divided plural society' in which 'domination' posed the 'basic dilemma'[23]. Earlier scholarly works within the liberal representation had proposed a 'separate but equal' strategy[24], and, later, a federation for Southern Africa in which, during a first stage, electoral arrangements such as a qualified franchise should be given serious consideration[25]. These were increasingly viewed as unacceptable since liberal scholars shared 'a deeply ingrained suspicion of the group as a political category'[26].

More recent liberal scholarly works aimed to extend liberal values - encapsulated in the idea of constitutionalism - in modern South African society. During the 1970s, the question of the process leading toward such an open pluralist society had become a salient issue. Marquard had already raised the idea of political negotiations, and scholars participating in the Study Project on Christianity in Apartheid Society (Sprocas) took the idea much further[27].

As was shown in the previous chapter, the liberal emphasis was on an evolutionary process of political negotiations aimed at establishing, over time, a common society. The point of departure of such a process, as defined in two influential liberal scholarly works in the 1970s[28], was modern South African society as a 'divided plural society'. The subject concerned political power, as vested in the government and the state. Both these works subjected this society to deep comparative analysis and thereby recognised its ethnic and cultural heterogeneity, together with its racial, class, and nationalist cleavages, the deep inequalities which these had fashioned, and the centralised nature of the minority White government.

It is the waning importance of this 'ethnic and cultural heterogeneity' in liberal scholarly works over the last fifteen years that is the subject here.

The major preoccupation of liberal political scientists during the period under scrutiny has been to address the unequal 'group' and racial character of the South African polity in terms acceptable to liberal, individualistic principles. This was done by proposing a consociational model as a basis for negotiation among all groups. This model comprises four principle elements[29]: a grand coalition of leaders of all significant groups in the country, a mutual veto, a system of proportionality (usually relating to electoral procedures), and segmental autonomy, often linked to a federal form of government. The purpose of the consociational model was, once a universal franchise was introduced, to avoid majoritarianism in government - to move away from the Westminster system - so as to enable democratic power-sharing. This could best be done, it was argued, in a constitutional system with strong (territorial) federal elements.

With regard to the process of establishing such a consociational democracy, Sprocas scholars proposed a first phase during which the sovereignty of the (all-White) South African parliament would not be affected, whilst - some six years later - Slabbert and Welsh excluded all reference to racial classification during any phase of their proposed process of introducing a universal franchise and consociational democracy[30].

It is clear from this latter work that it is the 'structural inequality of wealth, status and power', and the (morally and politically unacceptable) statutory racial system, and its roots in Afrikaner nationalism, rather than the potentially challenging ethnic heterogeneity of modern South African society, which were considered to be primary:

> The story of white politics and parties is really the story of how Afrikaner nationalism, despite obstacles and vicissitudes, could ultimately capture control of the political system and subject the entire society to its domination...
>
> Black nationalism in South Africa has never been a monolithic entity; rather, it has been a congeries of groups with different ideological, class and, perhaps, regional interests, held together by a common (and predominantly defensive) rejection of racial discrimination. Moreover, it may not be assumed that purely ethnic black parties (such as Tswana, Xhosa, etc.) would be wholly eclipsed in an open election, although it seems likely that support for them would be, relatively speaking, marginal. (Slabbert and Welsh 1979: 80,81,95,96)

As a result of these emphases, the major political challenges took the form of addressing massive state repression, of lessening the huge inequalities, and of evolution rather than revolution, with a view to establishing a non-racial government of a democratic nature[31]. In the late eighties, the essence of the South African situation, wrote Slabbert, 'is a struggle for power', in which a special emphasis on race and ethnicity is not primary[32].

Critics of this 'liberal democratic' approach to change in South Africa underlined the absence of attention paid to ethnic heterogeneity in its work:

> Liberalism has for the most part failed to recognize the legitimate aspects of mobilized ethnicity, by associating ethnicity solely with unfair advantage or the height of irrationality. But insofar as ethnicity expresses cultural distinctiveness and the quest for individual identity through group membership, it may fulfill desires that liberalism ignores. (Adam and Moodley 1986: 220)

> In the view of Slabbert and Welsh, the core of the South African conflict lies in inequality... Recent analyses of ethnic conflicts elsewhere show... (that), on the one hand, there is an interest component which, in divided societies, refers to the unequal access which the various ethnic groups have to resources. On the other hand, there is an emotional and identity component which refers to the need for communal or national identity, as expressed by political self-determination... These scholars issue a strong warning against exaggerating the influence of the materialist component in politics...
>
> In Africa, a liberal democratic government has invariably given rise to open ethnic competition. It has generally weakened democratic processes and it has

put the state at risk in many countries. (Giliomee and Schlemmer 1989b: 162,163,166)

Giliomee and Schlemmer, in the same work, put this waning of the importance of ethnicity in liberal thought down to the growing belief that constitutional proposals needed to be acceptable to the Black majority. 'Liberals had become apologetic, they had moved into retreat'[33]. In like vein, Arend Lijphart - a scholar who introduced the idea of consociationalism into the South African scholarly debate - wrote:

> There are good reasons for the opponents of the South African government both to dislike ethnicity and to think of race and ethnicity as equally objectionable concepts. Race and ethnicity have both been the tools of minority rule and the suppression of the majority... There are also good *political* reasons for those opposing the government to de-emphasize ethnicity. The National Party government mainly represents a single cohesive minority ethnic group - the Afrikaners - whereas the opposing majority is divided into a large number of ethnic groups. Since unity spells strength and division weakness, it is just as logical for the government to stress ethnicity as for the opposition to play it down. (Lijphart 1989: 14. Emphasis in the original)

Lijphart, a liberal political scientist, has remained a constant dissident voice with regard to what he called the 'end-of-ethnicity myth'. After carefully distinguishing, in South African society, between racial and ethnic divisions, he proposed a consociational model in which self-determined (in contradistinction to predetermined) ethnic representation is central. He was sympathetically critical of the mix of self-determined and predetermined (essentially racial) forms of ethnic representation in the proposed Natal Indaba[34] since he believed that individual choice should guide membership of ethnic groups in the political domain. He wrote as follows:

> My bottom line remains that complete self-determination of ethnicity is optional, that a combination of self-determination and carefully defined predetermination is acceptable, and that complete predetermination is unworkable and unacceptable in South Africa...
>
> Ethnicity and ethnic divisions are facts of life in South Africa. It is tempting to play down the ethnic factor both because it superficially appears to have been declining in importance during the last decades and because it would be much easier to find a democratic solution for South Africa if the country were a basically homogeneous or an only mildly divided society. Unfortunately... the latter image does not stand up to sober comparative scrutiny. South Africa's ethnic divisions cannot be wished away. (Lijphart 1989: 22,23)

By the early 1990s, liberal political scientists were deeply involved with the 'process' issues of political negotiations and political violence, and with 'social contract' issues in the fields of economics, land, and welfare. Lijphart's liberal voice[35] was one of the few which raised the issue of ethnicity in that arena.

To readers familiar with the modern scholarly literature on South African society, the fact that I have yet to classify and discuss the works of Heribert Adam may have come to mind. I will close this section with a short analysis of the ways in which he has addressed ethnicity in modern South African society.

Adam is difficult to place within one of the three scholarly representations developed earlier. His early work has been described as using an 'inherently conflictual' methodology by a liberal scholar[36] and his later work as using 'a broadly Weberian approach' by a marxist scholar[37]. He has produced numerous scholarly works on South African society over the past twenty years, and is frequently cited in the literature under scrutiny here.

Perhaps the best way to analyse his approach to the study of ethnicity is to start with his own analysis of this issue:

> Is South Africa, therefore, an intractable communal conflict, comparable to endemic strife in plural societies elsewhere? Or has it enough of a common society - with shared languages, Christian religious culture and consumerism - to bind its citizens together, provided equal political rights and opportunities are created?
>
> The answer depends in part on one's faith and optimism. Empirical and comparative historical evidence can be marshalled for either proposition.
>
> Making the assumption that ethnicity is a primordial given supports the pessimistic scenario: an intractable communal conflict. If politicized ethnicity, however, is construed as a fostered and manipulated attitude, an outlook dependent on circumstances, it is conceivable that even Afrikaners will shed their historical baggage when immersed in new structural realities and when ethnicity is muted through changing patterns of inter-group contact and interest-based association. (Adam 1990: 453,454)

In 1979, in a major work on South African society (Adam and Giliomee), Adam used the notion of ethnicity to analyse mobilisation strategies of Afrikaner nationalism. The notion is used broadly and in a changing historical context, sometimes as a synonym for nationalism, and particular emphasis was given to ethnic mobilizers, to elite manipulation, in the creation of ethnic identities.

In addition, it is worth noting that the work included a chapter criticising both liberal politics and the liberal scholarly representation of South African society (Ch. 9).

In 1986, in another major work[38], ethnicity was used in a more sophisticated manner. Black nationalism and Afrikaner nationalism were treated as central ideologies, and the work included a sympathetic analysis of the Inkatha movement. The main thrust of the work was to argue that, ethnic (and racial) identities notwithstanding, modern South African society contained sufficient shared values, liberal and individualistic institutions, and cross-cutting loyalties to enable a common society to emerge, provided that constitutionalism, particularly political rights for all citizens, was introduced.

In 1992, in a paper on the political conflict in Natal[39], 'faith and optimism' have faded. In search of a multi-causal explanation for the conflict, the authors wrote:

> Why has simmering ideological conflict been transformed into a tribal clash in the perceptions of its participants?.. An explanation need not recall historical competitions and conflicts between the two Nguni-speaking people (the Zulus and the Xhosas)... (Rather, it was) the independence strategy pursued by the *Inkatha* movement after 1979, not unrelated to Buthelezi's personality and statutory role... Tribal separateness was reinforced... by his divergent policies. (497,498)

This 'political mobilisation' approach, however, was qualified when the authors wrote:

> (C)hiefs, *indunas*, *sangomas*, and shack-lords present (the conflict) as a legitimate defense of a traditional order. Their large clientèle has little option other than to fall in line...
>
> The call for cultural revival is heeded because the most deprived among the Zulu people search for responses to their humiliation. An escape into a mythical (past) of pride and success in battle provides the dignity that most of the hostel dwellers and unemployed migrants have lacked. In this predicament, tribal loyalty carries with it a badge of honour. Only those with a more secure identity of a different kind consider the tribal collective to be a badge of shame. (500,501)

The authors reveal three attitudes to ethnicity in these latter passages. In the first place, they employ the notion of 'tradition' as an important source of ethnic identity. In the second place, they employ the term, tribe - indisputably, a pejorative term - to describe this form of traditionalism and, in the third place, they refer to an historical ethnic community in which myths of 'pride and success in battle' carry deep symbolic importance. These stances will be discussed in the next section. The authors concluded, as has already been mentioned in an earlier chapter, with a call for the careful consideration of 'a constitutionally entrenched right to secede' in the new South African dispensation[40].

History and ethnic community

Sociologists and political scientists are primarily concerned with contemporary processes and events. As we have seen, they have tended to address ethnicity on its first level, that of individual identity, and to address the role played by this identity in society in general, and in the political domain in particular. The second level of this conceptualisation, the cultural ideas and consciousnesses, and the histories, of what Anthony Smith called ethnic communities, more properly belongs to the discipline of history.

Three distinct sets of scholarly works - all undertaken during the 1980s - on the history of South African society will be analysed. Though interrelated, they have clearly differing aims. Each has been developed, moreover, within the marxist scholarly representation.

Marxist scholarship in the discipline of history arose out of a growing critique of liberal South African history. As was mentioned in the previous chapter, the initial major controversy revolved around relations between modern South African racial policy and its economic development[41]. Was South Africa's unique form of economic development driven by, and reinforced by, racial capitalism, or did urban-industrial development create conditions for the liberalisation of racial discrimination and, accordingly, of growing African resistance?

Numerous historical works[42] within the marxist representation were produced by this debate. Few addressed ethnicity. The three sets of work selected here are different. As we shall see, each developed a particular focus on ethnicity in South Africa. In this sense, they may be seen as exceptions within the larger set of marxist scholarly works on South Africa.

In a series of remarkable scholarly works, published by Ravan Press under the title: New History of Southern Africa Series, the changing nature and eventual demise of a number of pre-colonial, or pre-capitalist, societies in Southern Africa have been analysed. These included studies of the Xhosa, Pondo, Zulu, Swazi, Pedi, and Southern Tswana societies[43].

In the second place, a group of historians have introduced a focus on social and cultural life 'from below', focusing on the lives and perceptions of ordinary people, particularly in South African urban areas during the twentieth century[44].

A third initiative undertaken by marxist historians may be described as historical analyses addressing the ways in which stereotypes of ethnic identities and mythologies supposedly rooted in these pre-capitalist societies have been created, appropriated, and reinforced by different interest groups after the demise of these societies. It is rather - these historians argued - constructed or invented identities and consciousnesses which inform contemporary ethnic phenomena[45].

My primary aim in this section is to show that, as a consequence of the realist methodology and materialist form of analysis which guided marxist scholars, pre-colonial societies were understood mainly in terms of their pre-capitalist economies. As these economies were destroyed through capitalist market intrusions, members of these societies - it was argued - were not only incorporated into the emergent working class of modern South African society, but their fading cultures and their associated identities were increasingly replaced by class culture and class identity.

In so far as pre-capitalist ethnic identities and consciousnesses persisted, these were 'invented' and 'contrived' identities and consciousnesses, often manipulated by missionary and colonial representatives, and - in latter-day modern South Africa under its apartheid regime - often manipulated by apartheid ideologues. Accordingly, these identities and consciousnesses came to be viewed either as anomalous, and as harmful to newly proletarianising urban and rural communities, or - in Meillassoux's words - as no more than 'administrative inventions', shorn of 'living social' reality.

In attempting to show these trends in scholarly thought, I would like to acknowledge that there are important differences of emphasis to be found in these three sets of excellent historical studies. Accordingly, I will point to such variance on a number of occasions.

Pre-capitalist societies in South Africa

The use of a materialist form of analysis in the first set of works is apparent. In his study of the Pedi polity during the second half of the nineteenth century, Delius indicated the need for more materialist historiographical concerns. He wrote:

> Close attention (needs to be given) to the penetration of merchant capital, the impact of capitalist forms of production, and, in this context, the imposition of colonial rule...
>
> A second body of literature also... proved useful... This was produced by a growing school of economic anthropology in France which drew heavily on marxist theory and whose writings provided insights into the nature of power and the loci and forms of conflict in non-capitalist... societies. Their concern to identify and analyse 'modes of production' and 'social formations' led them along an increasingly holistic path, and to investigate not only economic relations and structures but also those of kinship, ideology and politics, and their inter-relationship... These writers also employed the articulation of modes of production. (Delius 1983: 5,6)

Similarly, in his work on the destruction of the Zulu kingdom, Guy wrote:

> (During the late nineteenth century), (t)he majority of the Zulu were still held firmly in the different production communities of the kingdom, moving from one type to another as they grew older and their status altered. The boys worked in their fathers' homesteads before establishing homesteads of their own, while the girls worked in their fathers' homesteads before establishing their own production units within their husbands' homesteads. Of course external forces had affected the Zulu increasingly as settler communities became established on the borders of the kingdom. Nevertheless throughout the reigns of the kings Zulu labour expended within the commoners' homesteads continued to support the bulk of the population, and the surplus which was drawn from them by the king... created the basis for his material power and authority. (Guy 1982: 18)

Two points about this realist approach may be made. The first is that materialist forces, economic forces within the pre-capitalist mode of production, were presented as the fundamental forces. Identities, consciousness, and the world of ideas were considered to be more superficial. The second point is that there was, accordingly, a theoretical implication that as one economic system made way for another, as the pre-capitalist mode of production was superseded by the capitalist mode, ideas and consciousness also changed, by taking on a working (or bourgeois) class character.

My formulation points to functionalist and reductionist logic. I will show that Guy, for example - in contradistinction to various other marxist scholars - analysed this issue in a more sophisticated fashion. Nevertheless, the theoretical implication remains valid. This may be shown by pointing to the theoretical importance these scholars attached to the 'dividing line' between a 'pre-capitalist' and 'capitalist world'. In this regard, Guy argued:

> Chiefs, husbands, and fathers can still retain ideological dominance even though the original material base for this dominance has disappeared and their authority is now linked with the circuit of capitalist production...
>
> To locate the features which warn us that we are leaving the pre-capitalist world we must search for fundamental changes in production and in accumulation... (in particular), fundamental technological change...
>
> Such a change never developed within South African pre-capitalist societies: instead, when they escaped destruction, they were restructured by external forces which selected certain pre-capitalist forms which were able to assist in this specific transition towards the capitalist mode of production. (Guy 1987: 36,37)

In fact, Guy concluded his work on the destruction of the Zulu kingdom with the following words: 'The Zulu nationalist movement today, whose leaders are in many cases the direct descendants of the men who fought the civil war, and who draw consciously on the Zulu past, is a force which will still affect the course of southern African history'[46]. (The quotation in Chapter III, taken from a later work by Guy, is also relevant here).

The scholarly influence of this materialist view of change in South Africa over the last hundred years has been illustrated in quotations given elsewhere, for example, Meillassoux's claim in the first chapter, and that of Maré and Hamilton earlier in this chapter. One more illustration may be given.

In a study of land dispossession in 1975 of a Sotho group in the Hershel district of the Eastern Cape, the following claim regarding a rapidly changing form of consciousness is made:

> Details of the Sotho's life in Herschel 'before the troubles' reveal a community living as a collective identity (*sic*), both economic and social. However, the past is at times characterized in an all too idyllic fashion, flattened out into a seemingly timeless recollection of happy and industrious events, untroubled by

intrusion from South Africa's struggles or, indeed, the cash economy. Nonetheless, these possibly idealistic memories are what the people live on, and as such have their own reality...

(T)he bantustan system has turned (these) conservative and pliant people into voices of opposition. In their tents in Botshabelo, the Herschelites have undergone a process of proletarianisation and marginalisation - they are now workers without jobs, peasants without land... They now speak a new language - the language of a future united and democratic South Africa...

(Cobbett and Nakedi 1988: 79,88)

'History from below'

Doreen Atkinson described and criticised the 'History from Below' group of scholars in the following terms:

A novel approach to history-writing emerged during the 1980s... (A) new generation of historians has begun to explore details of social and cultural life in South Africa. This new approach is important, because it has reacted against marxist theoretical abstractions, and instead emphasised the perceptions of ordinary people... Yet (this) genre of research is fatally based on a biased definition of what should count as the 'grassroots':

"Such a history should resonate with the lives of ordinary people rather than reflect the deliberations of the ruling classes..." (Bozzoli 1983: 8)

This extraordinary claim highlights these historians' *a priori* exclusion of members of 'the ruling classes' from the category of 'ordinary people'... This tradition is premised on historical materialism:

"(U)nless studies focusing on the local and small-scale retain concern for the wider process of class formation, capital accumulation and state strategy which impinge upon the smallest of communities in profound ways, they will degenerate into the anecdotal and the parochial" (Bozzoli 1983: 35).

(Atkinson 1991: 96,98)

When these studies identified ethnic (non-class) identities in the cases under study - and such identities were found[47] - they were explained within the marxist framework described above:

New arrivals in the city come from a variety of settings whose differences from each other frequently far outweigh any others they previously confronted. Furthermore because of the fact that proletarianisation varies regionally and with time, the arrival of groups from particular regions may occur in 'cohorts', differentiated temporally... (N)ot all (resulting) cleavages can be attributed to the machinations of capital or state...

Few of these cleavages can be properly understood without reference to the path *into* the proletariat which a particular group has followed...

For those who are not of the wealthier or better educated strata, the process of community-formation takes place mainly as a way of coping with the brutal fact of dispossession...(In such circumstances, community) lacks the timelessness, the permanence and the internal harmony which idyllic invocations of 'community' imply. (Bozzoli 1987: 23,24,26. Emphasis in the original.)

In one such study in which oral mineworker testimony was the main source of empirical evidence, Guy and Thabane considered the two dimensions of class and of ethnicity which they identified in this evidence to be 'contradictions':

a group of working men who responded to an urban, industrial commodity-producing environment by organising themselves on the grounds of their common, rural, tribal background; a group of men who were identified by their 'traditional' dress and weaponry, and who were named (it is said) after the Russians - feared victors in the recent 'European' war. (Guy and Thabane 1987: 442)

Two points about the approach used by this group of historians may be made. The first, flowing from its emphasis on phenomenology, on the gathering of information directly from the grassroots, 'from below', at it were, is that it did succeed in identifying, *inter alia*, ethnic identities and an ethnic consciousness in a number of urban categories.

The second point is that, by restricting its focus to the 'proletariat', by excluding the 'wealthier or better educated strata', it narrowed the analysis and, accordingly, excluded a number of possible explanations for the ethnic phenomena it had identified.

Consider as *hypotheses* the following two claims:

Cementing the ethnic division of labor is the preeminent role of ascriptive ties in the developing world. Family and close friends - certainly members of the same ethnic group - tend to be instrumental in locating economic opportunities for kinsmen. (Horowitz 1985: 110)

(E)conomic development and modernization may evoke ethnicization. Development does not eliminate ethnicity but makes for its refiguration. Different modes of modernization and development produce different forms of ethnic association and mobilization. (Pieterse 1993: 12.13)

Neither hypothesis, it seems to me, may be tested adequately within a methodology which proposes that proletarianisation is the fundamental process in a capitalist society, and which thereby excludes analyses of the role of (ethnic or other) elites in community studies.

In a study of the Industrial and Commercial Workers Union in the 1920s, Bradford moved out of the theoretical constraints of the 'history from below' approach when she wrote:

> Even when middle class blacks were drawn from households which had partially dissociated themselves from chiefdoms, they generally grew up speaking the language of a particular ethnic group, participating in some of its political and cultural practices, and acquiring a pantheon of its heroes who had resisted white conquest. Thus in addition to racial oppression, ethnic traditions could be used to elide class differences. (Bradford 1987: 64)

'The creation of tribalism'

In the previous chapter, it was shown that a new group of Afrikaner historians who had broken from the Afrikaner nationalist scholarly representation had defined this representation itself as a cultural and historical object of enquiry. Marxist historians working within their scholarly representation, have undertaken the same task with regard to conceptions of the histories of pre-capitalist African societies in South Africa.

John Wright, for example, in a work designed to show that the idea, 'Nguni' is simultaneously invented and ideologically functional for the maintenance of white minority rule in South Africa, began by stating that '(t)he word "Nguni" is today commonly used... for the black people who historically have inhabited the eastern regions of southern Africa from Swaziland through Zululand, Natal, the Transkei and the Ciskei to the eastern Cape'. He concluded this work with the following claim:

> As appropriated by South African scholars and administrators for their own specific purposes in the 1920s and 1930s, and as used in academic circles for the past fifty years, Nguni remains a political loaded term. Objectively its main ideological function appears to be to impose a primordial ethnic unity of the African peoples of the eastern seaboard of South Africa, and thus allow them collectively to be portrayed by their European-descended rulers as descendants of recent immigrants, with no more historically established rights to the region's resources than the offspring of immigrants from Europe... As a generic term... it has no historical validity. (Wright 1987: 96, 111)

In a similar claim regarding the ideological role of such systems of ideas,

Suttner asserted the following with regard to African customary law in modern South Africa:

> The Bantu law/ court system articulates with (the) wider policy of retribalization and helps maintain the 'tribal' family. Its continued viability is important if the patriarchal family production unit is to continue its subsidization of the capitalist mode of production.
>
> Ideologically, the special courts seek to constitute individuals as specific tribal subjects and this serves or seeks to splinter attempts at developing a national movement and/or national consciousness. It is sought to blur the contradiction between Africans and the white 'colonial bloc', through promoting specific tribal identities. (Suttner 1987: 133)

These two examples point to the role such ideological manipulations have played with regard to White and capitalist minority interests. A similar argument has been made with regard to the interests of the Inkatha movement, as reflected in its ideology:

> The Inkatha leadership has shaped and wrapped a political commodity which is being offered to various conservative takers in South Africa and internationally. This is clear in their language and their strategies. The wrapping makes the political package *appear* ambiguous, but the sales patter, upon examination, does not hide the conservative and repressive direction taken within the movement...
>
> Despite the populist rhetoric of unity and common interests Inkatha displays class political and economic interests that increasingly mesh openly with the forces of conservatism in South Africa... While clearly antagonistic towards the apartheid system and working towards its abolition, Inkatha has become an integral part of the system of ensuring the survival of capitalism in South Africa. (Maré and Hamilton 1987: 217,221 Emphasis in the original).

Two points may be made about these illustrations. The first is that the ideological dimension of the claims were primary, and that these ideologies were seen to serve other, sometimes hidden, purposes - in particular, the objective interests of White capitalism. The second point is simply that, as a result of this primacy, the ethnic identities of the individuals concerned were not conceived to be of importance, or, at the very least, not of significant importance.

In 1989, a number of marxist historians working on these questions collaborated to produce a collected study of the histories of various societies in Southern Africa[48]. Subsequently, this study has been typified, within the community of marxist scholars, as a major breakthrough in the study of ethnicity[49]. The second part of this section, accordingly, comprises an analysis of the ways in which ethnicity is analysed in the South African case studies within this wider study, in particular, in the four case studies relating to changing forms of African ethnic identity and consciousness in modern South African society.

In his introduction, Vail argued in favour of a major departure from established marxist models employed to address ethnicity:

> Ethnicity's future, even in countries such as South Africa, where industrialization has proceeded further than anywhere else on the continent, seems secure because it is likely to provide an important focal point for whatever opposition to the dominant political classes that might exist.
>
> (A)s ethnicity and parochial loyalties within the borders of nation states are likely to continue, it is important to cease approaching them from the perspective of the nation state itself. Ignoring them as embarrassing epiphenomena that should have long ago disappeared will do no good. Condemning them as 'reactionary' or 'divisive' will accomplish very little. (Vail 1989b: 2,17,18)

These guidelines have certainly informed the analysis in the four case studies under consideration:

Patrick Harries, in a study of the formation of ethnicity among the Tsonga-speaking people, concluded as follows:

> (E)thnicity should be seen in processual terms as the historical product of internal colonialism. But it has been stressed that ethnicity should not be seen in simple terms as the response, within one region, of a uniform class with identical interests to a situation of core-periphery exploitation and under-development. Ethnicity has emerged out of the acceptance and propagation by various classes of cultural symbols that cut across class barriers and distinguish and unite people as 'Tsonga'... The expression of an ethnic consciousness does not eradicate narrower loyalties to chief or clan; these can coexist with other feelings of class, national or religious consciousness. (Harries 1989: 110)

Shula Marks, in a chapter on the politics of Zulu consciousness which built upon substantial earlier works[50], wrote:

> The significance of Zulu ethnic associations and cultural nationalism in diffusing class-based organisations and fracturing national movements is no new phenomenon...
>
> In 1937, the Zulu Cultural Society was founded by Albert Luthuli, later to become President of the ANC and a winner of the Nobel Prize...

(This society's) own glorification of a Zulu cultural identity was as much shaped by elements of popular consciousness coming from below as it was a shaping force in the making of that consciousness... The problem for Africans in Zululand and Natal, however, was the ways in which a pre-colonial past provided military metaphors for mobilization. (Marks 1989: 216,217,233)

In a paper on ethnicity and 'pseudo-ethnicity' in the Ciskei, the author (who preferred to remain anonymous) concluded:

This chapter recognizes the existence of ethnic consciousness (in the Ciskei) as a real phenomenon which cannot be denied or otherwise wished away. Where there is competition for power or material resources, and where competing factions are able to stake out their claims in ethnic terms, such rival factions might seize on almost any aspect of language, history, culture or physical type and turn it into the criterion of ethnic difference. (Vail 1989a: 409)

Pseudo-ethnicity - the ideology of Ciskeian nationalism - is 'wholly bogus', this author argued, largely because 'the region which now forms part of the Ciskei has a deep-rooted historical tradition of fierce resistance to colonial domination which transcends ethnic boundaries and pre-colonial political structures and is now closely linked with a broad South African nationalism'[51].

In his study of the Swazi in Swaziland and the Transvaal, in comparable vein, Hugh Macmillan argued:

In Swaziland an exclusivist cultural nationalism has triumphed since independence in 1968, while in South Africa those who sought to mobilize the Swazi as a political force were confronted by formidable obstacles, in the shape not only of competing ethnicities but also of a broader based South African nationalism. (Macmillan 1989: 290)

Three separate points may be made about these studies. It is clear that ethnic phenomena are treated with much greater independence than was the case in earlier marxist works. In certain cases, ethnic identities were related to historically-relevant 'cultural symbols that cut across class-barriers', to 'a pre-colonial past' which provided 'military metaphors for mobilization'; in short, in Anthony Smith's terms, to aspects of 'ancient myths and old beliefs'. On the other hand, ethnicity was also presented as the political manipulation of 'almost any aspect' of contemporary individual identities, an approach reminiscent of Roosens' view (identified in Chapter III) of ethnic identity as fundamentally elastic. Though lacking consensus between these scholars, both levels of ethnicity did emerge from their work.

The second point relates to Vail's plea that such studies should cease to address ethnicity at the level of the 'nation state'. We have seen that there are strong theoretical pressures (within each of the dominant scholarly representations) to maintain such a focus, a focus on the macro-level. In the case studies under consideration here, such a focus - Vail's plea notwithstanding - was explicit. It is located in the notion of a 'broad South African nationalism', a primary notion in the analyses of Marks, the author of the chapter on the Ciskei, and Macmillan. This nationalism is 'fractured' by Zulu ethnic consciousness. It 'transcends' attempts to create a bogus Ciskeian ethnic consciousness, and it creates 'formidable obstacles' for those who sought to 'mobilise the Swazi'. It serves as the broader South African counterpoint to all narrower exclusivist ethnic representations.

This point is worth pursuing. What is this 'broad South African nationalism' to the scholars we are discussing? What is its common myth of descent, its shared history, its distinctive shared culture, its sense of solidarity? And, if Anthony Smith is correct in also pointing to the need for a collective name, what is its name? Was Calpin wrong when, in 1941, he chose - as title for his well-known book - the claim that 'There are no South Africans'? We have seen that there is no scholarly representation of South African nationalism. Scholars have not written its history. They have not identified and analysed its culture. Neither have they referred to other scholars who have attempted to do so. The notion is without scholarly input. It refers at best to the notion of 'territorial nationalism'[52], to the ideology of nation-building in a plural society.

On the other hand, the narrow, exclusivist, ethnic representations are precisely the objects of enquiry which these marxist historians have selected for study. They do have collective names, common myths of descent, distinctive shared cultures, solidarities. These are neither fixed nor given. They have been reconstituted and manipulated, reinvented and moulded, but they have been shown to be real in the minds of the individuals concerned. Distasteful though they may well be to some scholars, they have been identified and analysed.

In short, the broader South African counterpoint is no more than a political ideology (albeit one which produces real consequences), whilst the narrower exclusivist ethnicities point to communities, changing in different ways at different times but representations nonetheless of the present and of the past which are meaningful to those that carry them. To compare the two is unreasonable. To invoke the first and to disparage the second is simply ideological, without scholarly legitimation in terms of felt identities of South Africans[53].

That exclusivist traditionalism is distasteful to the scholars concerned is clear. Marks concluded her chapter by referring to 'contemporary "tribal" violence' in Natal[54] Macmillan referred to Whites and Blacks pressing for 'retribalization'[55], and Vail selected, for the collected study, the disparaging title *The Creation of Tribalism in Southern Africa*. Guy now uses the term[56], as do Adam and Moodley, as I indicated earlier in this chapter. That the term, tribalism is pejorative in contemporary South African society is without doubt. By using it, these scholars signal moral judgement, perhaps even condemnation of these ethnic communities and their particularistic values. In choosing this title, Vail disregarded his own admonishment that condemnation would 'accomplish very little'.

Patrick Harries[57] did not enter into this ideological and judgemental mode of analysis in his work. He did not counterbalance Tsonga ethnicity against 'South African nationalism', nor did he use the term 'tribe'. His analysis of leadership in Gazankulu under the apartheid government is both empathetic and critical. His chapter is the exception among the case studies considered in this section.

In the third place, terms such as 'traditionalism', and such as 'loyalties' to 'chief', to 'clan', and to 'tribe', are still widely interpreted within a general theory of modernisation. The implication seems to be that as this process unfolds, these 'parochial' loyalties will tend to dissolve.

Recent scholars of ethnicity are increasingly insistent that this view is insufficient, if not invalid. 'Modernity and ethnicity coexist very well. Development does not eliminate ethnicity but makes for its refiguration'[58]. 'Whereas ethnic conflicts were conceived earlier as a vestige destined to change and then as a vestige stubbornly resistant to change, recent theories of conflict view it as no vestige at all, but as part and parcel of the very process of becoming modern'[59]. These scholars imply, accordingly, that it is not only this theory, but also this terminology which needs to change.

Anthropology and ethnos

The review I will present in this section will cover familiar ground. It will identify the ways in which the three dominant scholarly representations have guided anthropologists in their work. It will also uncover methodologies and arguments already discussed within these representations, and it will - most importantly - show that the study of ethnicity was largely put to one side. (Except for studies executed within the Afrikaner nationalist representation), the focus of anthropological work gave primacy to social, economic, and political issues, and proposed that cultural issues were dependent on, were functional to, these other issues.

The discipline of anthropology in South Africa was initially deeply influenced by the structural functionalist approach of British anthropology. This approach was criticised by influential anthropologists of the time, such as Max Gluckman, for its 'timeless functionalism'[60]. In addition, South African anthropologists, notably J Clyde Mitchell and others at the Rhodes-Livingston Institute, pioneered new anthropological approaches in countries to the north of South Africa though the influence of this work in South Africa waned, as I will show later in this section. The influence of the structural functionalist approach, however, persisted and played an important role in the establishment, in the 1960s, of the theory of the plural society. The 'parts' of the 'plural' society could be envisaged as social and cultural 'systems', meeting in a 'common market-place'. This scholarly influence, accordingly, fed into the development of the liberal scholarly representation.

Volkekunde ('the study of cultures'), on the other hand, was an approach rooted in idealist German anthropological theories dating from before the Second World War. These theories proposed what John Sharp[61] has called a ultra-primordialist definition of 'ethnos', of ethnic community. This approach guided Afrikaner nationalist anthropologists at most Afrikaans universities in South Africa[62]. It conceptualised ethnic groups as cultural isolates, sharing 'a common language, system of knowledge, social structure, political and military structure, legal system, economy, educational system, games and technical and art forms'[63]. In short, it conceptualised an ethnic group as a *volk*, as a nation; or as a *volk-in-wording*, as an emergent nation.

As has been the case with other scholarly communities, the South African anthropological community, during the last fifteen years, fragmented into three separate parts:

> South African anthropology does not present a uniform front... Those who claim to be *volkekundiges* evince... a strong conservative tendency; contemporary social anthropologists within South Africa have a tradition of political liberalism... Those within South Africa who profess a radical anthropology can be counted on the fingers of one hand (although more South Africans of this persuasion practice outside the country)... (Sharp 1980: 3)

A large and impressive body of anthropological work has been produced during this period: rural poverty studies in many parts of the country[64], studies of resettlement in homelands[65], studies of betterment state programmes[66], studies of migration[67], and many others. Few of these studies addressed the issue of ethnicity. Rather, the main questions revolved around the effects of the developing capitalist economy, of changing state policies, and - since most studies addressed African communities - around the effects of imposed racial categories on members of these communities.

One of the most influential anthropologists during this period was Philip Mayer. Working within the liberal scholarly representation, his work addressed ethnicity directly. In 1975, he argued as follows:

> So far, at least in the South African context, topics like race, class, and ethnicity have been discussed without systematic attention being paid to the subjective angle, the people's own perceptions. It seems a major omission.
> (Mayer 1975: 142)

In the same work which addressed this 'subjective angle' with regard to permanent ('Section 10') residents of Soweto, Mayer made the following claims:

> (E)xclusive tribal patriotism seems to have died in Soweto... Ideologically, it is race and class oppositions that are claimed to matter, while ethnic oppositions are denied or simply shrugged off. This is one of the most clear cut findings in the whole mass of research material...
>
> Here then is one of the notable differences between Black urbanism in Soweto and in many other African cities... First, the Soweto rank and file interpret relations with Whites in terms of economic class... Second, in the social world of the Blacks themselves, class distinctions are largely seen as more important than ethnic ones... Third, the long experience of Blacks' living together has accelerated the processes of cultural integration within the townships. (Mayer 1975: 152,155)

It is probable that Mayer's analysis here, of the African ideology he called 'that of the melting pot'[68], was influenced by his earlier work which had identified, as a basic cleavage in the identities of African South Africans, the 'Red'-'School' divide, the consciousness either of being a 'tribesman' or of being a 'townsman'[69]. It is sufficient, however, simply to note the underlying liberal theory of modernisation as essentially assimilatory with regard to cultural differences.

This claim that cultural assimilation was taking place on a general basis was echoed in anthropological works on African separatist churches, a long-standing object of scholarly enquiry:

> Independent church members are bound together by common experience of adversity. They share also a background of a rural birthplace and a move to the city as young adults. This shared background and experience would seem to be sufficient to counteract any language or ethnic barriers that might have existed... and makes assimilation of new members relatively easy irrespective of ethnic affiliation. (West 1975: 84)

By 1980, Mayer's liberal approach had shifted toward a more marxist representation. In a series of essays addressing anthropological perspectives on labour migration, Mayer pointed to the rise of the 'resistance ideology' of 'Africanism', a claim that a form of racial and class consciousness was emerging, and asserted:

> Until the late 1960s or early 1970s, rural populations with the same ethnic background... were divided into communities of Red people... and of School people...
>
> The new 'sophisticated, aware, demanding men' from the homelands... (now) experience processes of individualization, secularization, and rationalization - manifestations of their also being absorbed, culturally and ideologically, by the capitalist society to which economically they have been subservient for a century, though they partially continued to practice pre-capitalist modes of production at home. (Mayer 1980: 1,68)

The influence of the marxist scholarly representation is evident in the works of other anthropologists. In the same collected work, McAllister analysed the religious behaviour of returned migrants in a rural Transkeian community. He concluded as follows:

> A man's rural home and community provide him with status and dignity not obtainable elsewhere, with full human relations unlike the fragmented and uncertain links in town or mine, and the ancestor cult affords him a sense of continuity, belonging and moral satisfaction. His 'conservatism', then, is an

ideology, a response to domination and subordination; an ideology which persists *because* of the conditions regulating the participation of migrants in the dominant economy, and which has 'tradition' and 'custom' as its point of reference, but which is not itself wholly 'tradition'. (McAllister 1980: 250 Emphasis in the original)

In more direct fashion, Spiegel argued:

Class formation is indeed taking place in the southern African periphery examined as a whole and including especially the Bantustans... Within these peripheral 'units' we can see the reproduction of capitalist relations at all levels - and thus the formation of antagonistic classes. But in the rural communities, differentiation is not an indication of class formation alone, primarily because of its cyclical nature. (Spiegel 1980: 161)

There was, however, one fundamental institution in the South African economy which troubled the growing anthropological consensus that exclusivist ethnicity was waning. It was the South African mining sector. In the few studies which focused on 'inter-group violence' on mines, the persistence of ethnic cleavages, as defined by participants themselves, was vexing to scholars. We have already witnessed an example earlier in this chapter[70]. MacNamara sought insights from anthropological works undertaken by British anthropologists elsewhere in Africa[71] to analyse 'the relatively unusual strength of ethnic cleavages on gold mines in South Africa'[72]. The issue remained unresolved[73].

The insignificant influence of recent British anthropological work on ethnicity in Africa - some undertaken by South Africans - is relevant. Mayer, as we have seen above, argued that the South African urban situation was different from that elsewhere in Africa. In so doing, his references to this body of British scholarly work were explicit. Sharp, in his seminal article on ethnicity in South Africa[74], was sharply critical of Barth's eclectic approach to situations of 'multi-ethnicity'. He then called for an approach to ethnicity firmly situated within the context of the 'political economy' of South Africa. In both cases, it would seem, there was a call for anthropology addressing modern South Africa society to follow a road different from other established roads, because this society was different from other societies.

During the late 1980s, the vexing ethnic question began to re-appear in the community of anthropologists. In 1987, Andrew Spiegel called for a re-examination by anthropologists of this question[75]. Emile Boonzaaier, John

Sharp and other South African anthropologists, in a work employing a similar approach to that used in this chapter, critically surveyed the ambivalent and politically loaded South African terminology relating to ethnicity[76]. And, in 1990, Deborah James, in a work directly addressing ethnic identities in a rural Lebowa village, argued as follows:

> It may seem puzzling that the challenge of applying (British anthropological) insights to South African anthropological studies was not taken up sooner. The reason... probably lies in the reluctance of these scholars, by acknowledging the existence of ethnic consciousness, to be thought of as endorsing the ideological underpinnings of apartheid. In addition, a number of anthropologists were using radical or materialist theory to help them understand the transformations wrought upon contemporary rural or urban communities in South Africa. While such an approach would definitely preclude the notion of ethnic affiliations as something primordial, it seemed equally incompatible with the writings of an author like Barth, whose 'methodological individualist' perspective emphasized the power of common people to manipulate social situations to their own benefit, and seemed naive in the light of the massive structural inequalities in South African society. (James 1990: 34)

The anthropological terrain sketched above, accordingly, is strikingly similar to the terrains covered for other social science disciplines in South Africa during the same period. This similarity includes recognition, in the late 1980s and early 1990s, of the need to change, to begin to address ethnicity more centrally in scholarly works.

It is fitting to close this section with a reference to the anthropological works of the Comaroffs, work primarily concerned with the Tswana people of Southern Africa. In a series of publications during the 1970s and 1980s[77], these authors developed a social constructivist approach to culture and history, an approach which focused upon the construction and reconstruction, over time, of integrated orders of symbols and practices[78]. These works, radical for their time and representing a counter-current to main-stream liberal and marxist anthropological works in South Africa, have become increasingly influential in the 1990s.

NOTES

1. See, for example, Bozzoli 1987, du Toit and Giliomee 1983, Grobbelaar 1991, Marks and Trapido 1987, Moodie 1974, Rhoodie and Couper 1986, Thompson 1985.
2. See, for example, Bekker 1975a, 1977, Kinloch 1972, Kuper and Smith 1969, Slabbert and Welsh 1979, Sprocas 1973, van den Berghe 1964, 1967.
3. See, for example, Adam and Giliomee 1979, Bekker 1975b, Boulle 1984, Horowitz 1985, Rex 1971, Schlemmer 1977.
4. See, for example, Kuper in Kuper and Smith 1969.
5. Adam and Giliomee 1979: 45.
6. The literature is enormous. See, for example, Lipton 1985, Urban Foundation 1989, 1990, Wilson and Ramphele 1989.
7. Again, the literature is enormous. See, for example, Giliomee & Schlemmer 1989a, 1989b, Schrire 1990, Slabbert & Welsh 1979, Thompson & Butler 1975.
8. Schrire 1990.
9. Three chapters (out of 24) are exceptions: that on language, by Neville Alexander, a marxist scholar, which will discussed subsequently, and those by Arend Lijphart on electoral systems and by Heribert Adam which will be discussed separately in this section.
10. van der Horst 1981.
11. The 1985 incidents took place in Malukazi (Bekker and Manona 1992) and Inanda (Cross et al. 1992(b)). The Midlands and Durban conflict is described in Bekker 1992.
12. Marks and Andersson: 54f.
13. Marks has discussed the conflict situation in the Natal Region in an ethnic context. This discussion is analysed later in this chapter.
14. Manganyi and du Toit 1990.
15. Kane-Berman 1990b: 65.
16. See, for example, Indicator South Africa, 50th edition, 1992.
17. See, for example, Coetzee 1989, an influential undergraduate text book.
18. The author was a member of the first department during the period mentioned, and was external examiner, in 1990, for the second.
19. Cloete 1981: 34.
20. Oral communication, Conference on Ethnicity, Identity and Nationalism, Rhodes University, Grahamstown, April 1993
21. Rhoodie and Couper 1986.
22. HSRC 1985: 5.
23. Sprocas 1973: 126.
24. de Beer 1961: 59f.
25. Marquard 1971: 126f.
26. Sprocas 1973: 126.
27. See Marquard Ch.10 and Sprocas Chs 11-13.
28. Slabbert and Welsh 1979, Sprocas 1973.
29. Boulle 1984: Ch.3.
30. Sprocas 1973: 230; Slabbert and Welsh 1979: 153.
31. Kane-Berman 1990b, Slabbert 1989: Ch.9
32. Slabbert 1989: 82; Slabbert 1990: 113.
33. Giliomee and Schlemmer 1989b: 160.
34. See, for example, Indicator South Africa 1987.
35. The theory of (and, indeed, the term) consociationalism, like others in the social sciences, was co-opted by apartheid ideologues during the 1970s and 1980s. As a result, this theory - for non-scholarly reasons - has lost sapiential authority in certain South African circles. For sympathetic comment on this issue, see Young 1986: 452,453; for critical comment see Dubow 1993: 14,15.
36. Atkinson 1991: 69.
37. Dubow 1993: 10.

38. Adam and Moodley 1986.
39. Adam and Moodley 1992.
40. Adam and Moodley 1992: 510.
41. For example, Davenport 1978, Leftwich 1974, Lipton 1985, Wright 1977.
42. The literature is large. See, for instance, Greenberg 1980, 1987, Marks and Trapido 1987, Simson 1980, Wolpe 1988.
43. See, for example, Delius 1983, Guy 1982,1987, Peires 1981, Shillington 1985.
44. Bozzoli 1983, 1987, 1992.
45. See, for example, Harries 1989, 1992, Macmillan 1989, Maré and Hamilton 1987, Marks 1986, 1989, Ranger 1983, Vail 1989a, 1989b, Wright 1987, 1989.
46. Guy 1982: 246.
47. See, for example, papers by Guy, Nicol and Webster in Bozzoli 1987.
48. Vail 1989a
49. See, for example, Guy 1992, Wright 1992.
50. See, for example, Marks 1986.
51. Vail 1989a: 396.
52. Giliomee 1991: 67.
53. In this regard, Lawrence Schlemmer has recently asserted that "'t)here is a not uncommon view, expressed without much thought but with an abundance of goodwill, that South Africa is reaching the threshold of a united, non-racial democracy... There are also people who believe in fairies and Father Christmas...' (Schlemmer 1992: 7)
54. Marks 1989: 234.
55. Macmillan 1989: 297.
56. Guy 1992.
57. Harries 1989.
58. Pieterse 1993: 12.
59. Horowitz 1985: 101. For examples within the community of scholars addressing South African society, see, for example, Degenaar 1993: 18, Giliomee and Schlemmer 1991b: 166, Lijphart 1989: 20.
60. Macmillan 1992.
61. Sharp 1980: 4.
62. Gordon 1989.
63. Kies 1978, as quoted in Sharp 1980: 5.
64. A large number of these works are listed in the bibliography of Bekker et al. 1993.
65. See, for example, Bank 1989, S.P.P. 1983.
66. See, for example, Cross and Haines 1988.
67. See, for example, Cross et al. 1992 (a),(b),(c), (d), Mayer 1980.
68. Mayer 1975: 153.
69. Mayer and Mayer, 1974.
70. Guy and Thabane 1987.
71. Epstein 1978.
72. MacNamara 1980: 337.
73. Shanafelt 1991.
74. Sharp 1980.
75. Oral communication, Workshop on Decision-making in Rural Areas, organised by DBSA, Johannesburg, Nov. 1987.
76. Boonzaaier and Sharp 1988.
77. See, for example, the bibliography in J. Comaraoff 1985.
78. See Kiernan 1987.

The Entire Image

Imagine a darkened canvas in need of restoration. To get an impression of the image that could emerge, one could begin with the few remaining bright spots, where the figures are clear, and work outwards, or scan first the indistinct edges, to get a sense of the boundaries of the entire image, and work inwards. (These are two approaches to a survey) of research on ethnicity and race...
(Alba 1991: 35)

Overview

In the preceding five chapters, I have tried to sustain a single theme: over the last fifteen years, scholars of modern South African society have argued - against the emerging standard practice of scholars studying other plural societies - that South African society is different, and, accordingly, needs to be analysed by employing ideas other than ethnicity.

In Chapter II, I pointed to this emerging standard practice - incomplete though it surely is - among scholars studying other plural societies. In Chapter III, I discussed ethnicity in a manner potentially applicable to modern South African society. This discussion was developed by using international comparative scholarship, and by distinguishing between the basic ideas scholars have used to study South African society, and the notion of ethnicity.

In Chapter IV, I identified the claim that South African society is different, and, simultaneously, the claims - within the three dominant scholarly representations of this society - that analysis requires ideas other than ethnicity to understand this society. In Chapter V, I argued that intellectual reasons alone were insufficient for a proper understanding of these claims. There were, in fact, also social, cultural and moral attributes of the community of scholars which led to these claims.

Finally, in Chapter VI, by way of a careful selection of scholarly works in which one could anticipate that the issue of ethnicity would emerge as important, I demonstrated that ethnic phenomena were generally treated as unimportant, as dependent upon more important forces, and - when they were identified empirically - were generally treated as anomalous and harmful to a new form of universalistic consciousness which, some scholars claimed, was emerging in modern South African society.

There are two aspects of my thematic treatment of these scholarly works which need to be emphasized. The first is that - such shared intellectual features notwithstanding - these works are all highly contested within the community of scholars studying South African society. Not only does this contestation reflect an international problem for the social sciences, but the dominance of the different scholarly representations during the fifteen years under consideration has altered. Afrikaner nationalist scholarship has gone into sharp decline and marxist scholarship has been in the ascendance. Liberal scholarship has accordingly needed to shift its focus from the former to the latter scholarly challenge.

It is evident that the reasons for this shifting dominance of scholarly representations need to be found not only in the intellectual claims within each representation, but also in the changing circumstances both within South African society and within the international community. The second aspect of the main theme of this work, therefore, is this fact, that a history of scholarly ideas cannot be divorced from the social environment within which it takes place, both the immediate social environment of the community of scholars and the wider social environment within which these scholars find themselves.

Ethnic studies eclipsed

In a recent study of ethnicity in South African society, the author pointed to the difficulties generally encountered by scholars who wish to analyse ethnicity in plural societies. 'As is common in divided societies, there is a belief (in South Africa) that talking about ethnicity creates or reinforces ethnic divisions... even when the talk is directed at how to prevent such divisions from overwhelming a future democratic state'[1].

As identified in Chapter V, the social, cultural and moral pressures on scholars of South African society - particularly on South African scholars - reinforced such a belief. A number of examples have already been cited in previous chapters. Tony Mathews admitted a 'reluctance' to acknowledge the potential for ethnic conflicts. Jeff Guy conceded the need to address ethnicity even though this may give the question 'unwarranted status', and deflect the debate from 'the essential problem of the deeper forces which create and exploit' it. Deborah James recognised that scholars were 'reluctant' to acknowledge 'the existence of ethnic consciousness', since this may be seen as endorsing 'the ideological underpinnings of apartheid'. And Arend Lijphart pointed not only to moral reasons underlying the evasion of addressing ethnicity, but also to political reasons: 'it is just as logical for the (South African) government to stress ethnicity as for the opposition to play it down'[2].

In the light of Lijphart's comment, it is appropriate to add to these social, cultural and moral pressures, a distinct political pressure. We have seen that liberal scholars became 'apologetic to the Black majority'. We have also seen that marxist scholars often became committed political supporters of the exile movements. These attitudes resulted in the development of a culture of 'political correctness', an orientation which led to the avoidance or evasion of ethnicity for political motives. These attitudes also resulted in the disparagement of ethnic movements where and when they emerged. The increasingly common use of the pejorative term, tribe, is ample evidence[3].

South African scholars' use of terminology may be used as a concluding example. As used in this book (and in most other recent relevant scholarly works), the terms Black and White are underpinned by a political paradigm: that of signaling shared identities among all South Africans who have suffered by virtue of discriminatory racial classification during the apartheid era ('Black'), and among those who enjoyed preferential treatment during the same era ('White'). This use implies - without evidence - that such shared identities are real (or emergent), and that potential shared identities within or across the Black and White categories are less likely to emerge. Though some scholarly work has been undertaken which addresses ethnicity within communities classified as 'Coloured' and as 'Indian', for example, their frequency appears to have decreased over the past fifteen years. The use of such terminology discourages meaningful discussion of ethnicity in contemporary South African society.

South Africa in transition

That all South Africans are caught up in a process of rapid political transition is well-known. That this process is affecting their lives in domains far beyond the formal political arena is increasingly known: international ties in the areas of trade, sport, tourism, and foreign relations are examples. Scientific, technical, cultural and academic exchanges are proliferating. Contacts with an increasing number of African countries, sometimes established for the first time, are being extended.

Within the country, political negotiations aimed at designing a new national constitution vie for public attention with attempts to regulate mounting conflict; with attempts to formulate policies for a democratic, post-apartheid South Africa; and - over the longer term - with attempts to agree on strategies aimed at improving the current gloomy material conditions of, and wide-ranging inequalities among, South Africans. And each of these issues vies, in turn, with discussions on interim strategies ('pacts' and 'charters') intended to introduce practical measures during the interim phase of transition.

A number of specific national challenges have emerged from this series of intense debates: the nature and scope of poverty in the country, and ways to address it; the challenge of urban reconstruction and its allied needs for shelter, education, and job creation; the salience of a youth culture and the part played by its alienated 'lost generation'; and, in rural areas, the land question: how to redistribute land to address historical inequities whilst simultaneously improving agricultural production. And, since each of these issues reflects pervasive racial inequalities in the country, there is the challenge of dismantling the current racial order and transforming the current racist state ideology in the country.

These welfare questions are complemented by debates on wealth creation which revolve around priorities relating to the promotion of exports or of 'inward industrialisation', around changing relationships between management and labour, around the role which large corporations in the private sector may play in the future, and around strategies to raise foreign loans for national reconstruction and infrastructural development.

A number of challenges regarding the new state and the new national constitution have also emerged: in which ways are state security forces - the police and the military - able to improve their credibility and efficiency, and to involve more Blacks in their ranks; in which ways are city governments and national state departments able to do the same; and in which ways will homeland administrations be incorporated into new state structures? And, at the level of national political negotiations, will the new constitution be clearly unitary or will it include federal elements? Will the nature of government be majoritarian or based on shared power? Will the process succeed in involving most political actors? And will the process succeed in establishing an interim government with sufficient legitimacy to develop a credible and viable constitution?

Finally, it is worth noting that these debates take place in a milieu in which violence, conflict, and crime are all perceived to be intensifying. Interpretations for this upsurge vary widely and each is highly contested. Many of the policy debates are influenced by these circumstances, thereby creating a context which often complicates the search for agreement between the different parties involved. Accordingly, the dominant sentiment is that these various national policy challenges need to be addressed urgently. This urgency moreover is underlined by the continuing deterioration of the present national and international economic climates.

There are two features of these debates on transition that of direct relevance to this work. The first is the manner in which the major challenges facing South African society are expressed. As a scholar directly involved in a number of these debates, I have attempted to reflect the definitions of the challenges as accurately as possible[4]. These definitions are virtually all couched in the language of the liberal and marxist scholarly representations. These definitions are built around the scaffold of 'race', 'class' and 'state'. Nationalism, particularly in its exclusivist Afrikaner or recent exclusivist Zulu senses, is viewed as a divisive factor. Other forms of nationalism are feared.

The second feature is that a number of processes have emerged in South African society which have brought ethnicity to the fore.

Whether as a result of the ideologies and changing policies of exclusivist Afrikaner nationalist or of ethnic African political movements, or as a result of the ethnic self-identification by participants in a sustained series of incidents, conflict and violence in the society are widely perceived to be taking on an ethnic character[5].

Simultaneously, as the process of national constitutional negotiations unfolds, issues which are also perceived to relate directly to ethnicity have emerged. Two are prominent. In the continuing debate on the form of the new South African state, unitary, federal or mixed options have forced debate on ethnicity to emerge, particularly in regard to the definition of regions, and justifications for the boundaries of these regions. In like measure, discussion on the country's future language policy have also led to such debates[6].

In short, though established scholarly representations of modern South African society continue to be used in addressing the challenges of transition, recognition of the growing importance of ethnicity is apparent. This leads scholars into a grave dilemma since their representation of modern South African society has not prepared them for these new, (in their view) generally undesirable, phenomena.

Ways to revive the scholarly debate on ethnicity

In calling for a revival of the ethnic debate in modern South African society, I do not imply that the major challenges identified above should be considered to be less important than they are at present. To the contrary, I imply that the ways these challenges are being addressed, and will be addressed in the future, may be understood better if ethnic identities and ethnic consciousnesses - where they exist or are emerging - are taken into account.

The call, accordingly, is to add ethnicity to the existing core scaffold of ideas which scholars have developed to understand modern South Africa. That challenges relating to the establishment of new state structures are crucial is self-evident. That challenges relating to class cleavages, class consciousness, and inequality will persist is equally self-evident. And, as Douwes Dekker has recently shown[7], that racial consciousness persists in South African communities is a distasteful and challenging constraint on the development of a democratic culture within the society.

The addition of ethnicity to this scaffold of ideas implies that scholarly work needs to be undertaken both at the level of ethnic identity and at the level of ethnic community. As we have seen in Chapter VI, such work has already begun.

In this regard, it is instructive to consider the pleas of scholars who are involved in such research elsewhere. Hobsbawm, for example, argues that 'there is no denying that "ethnic" identities which had no political or even existential significance until yesterday... can acquire a genuine hold as badges of group identity overnight'. He then proposes that 'these short-term changes and shifts of ethnic identity' constitute 'the area of national studies in which *thinking and research are most urgently needed today*'[8]. Noiriel has proposed similar arguments in relation to historical and political scholarship in France[9].

Anthony Smith's plea is both fervent and equally direct:

> To grasp the forms and intensity of (national) conflicts, we need knowledge and understanding of each community's *ethno-history*, the shared memories and beliefs of the members of the particular *ethnies*, and of the cultural activity of the community's intelligentsia. Most of all, we need to explore the continuing impact of ethnic myths, symbols and traditions of popular consciousness, and the way they continue to condition attitudes and behaviour to immigrants, minorities and outsiders, even in the most apparently rationalist and pragmatic societies...
>
> Research in this field is essential if we are to begin to understand, and so perhaps to ameliorate, the many social and political problems in the area. For to imagine that we can address such deep-rooted problems by often *ad hoc* economic or political means is to ignore at our peril the underlying conditions of such conflicts. (Smith 1992: 451. Emphasis in the original)

One further aspect of the scholarly debate on ethnicity in modern South Africa needs to be raised. We have seen that the community of South African scholars is overwhelmingly White, and its members generally belong to an international Anglophone culture. Few of these scholars speak the home languages of most Africans, and very few have a deep understanding of the differing processes of socialisation of their fellow African compatriots. The case for the rapid development of a larger Black, and particularly African, representation in this community of scholars is obvious.

Simultaneously, there is a need to create a research environment in which the scholarly study of ethnicity is considered to be both acceptable and valuable. This is no easy task, as many a South African scholar would admit. In an article on ethnicity in Africa, Shaw wrote of the 'unpopularity of the concept among both political practitioners and scientists.' Crawford Young, in his retrospective on scholarship on Africa, echoed these thoughts. Ethnicity, he wrote, is widely regarded as 'a retrogressive and shameful' topic. This view is shared 'not only by ruling classes but also by the African intelligentsia. There are special risks for an African scholar to engage in ethnicity research in a direct sense...' And Vail, in his collected work on the histories of Southern African societies in which ethnicity is considered to play a central role, remarked that 'although I canvassed African academics widely for papers... not a single one would undertake the writing of a paper which might be seen as "subversive" to the goal of political "nation-building"'[10].

The challenge

In the early 1990s, all South Africans find themselves caught up in fundamental change, in an 'historical moment', in what is probably the most important collective event of their lives. This change toward a new South Africa will be partially of their own and their leaders' making. In so far as their identities and their images of their communities and their society are important to them during this historical moment, these will influence, and may deeply affect, the outcome of this moment. These identities and images, in fact, will influence, and may deeply affect, the primary challenges - as presently defined - facing the society. Hence, the need to address ethnicity in its many forms so as to understand better the complexities of contemporary South African society. And, since international scholarship on the subject is rudimentary, scholars of South Africa need to approach this challenge with humility and need to avoid overhasty strategies which may be based upon little more than fashionable academic approaches or personal preferences.

As to nationalist tendencies - tendencies claiming sovereignty for 'nations' - in contemporary South African political ideologies, it is clear that the issue is both fundamental and highly controversial. Horowitz's judgement is that 'ethnicity is one of those forces that is community-building in moderation, community-destroying in excess'[11]. In contemporary South Africa, this - in my view - implies that all forms of exclusivist nationalism (which will become excessive) are potentially 'community-destroying'. In like measure, attempts to create a single South African nation in the sense of aiming to create a single transcendent South African culture and community run great risks of becoming excessive, and hence 'community-destroying'.

Doornbos observes that:
> *ethnic* pluralism and co-existence - as Africa has in fact known for most of remembered time in most of its regions - would require and presuppose a give-and-take attitude on the part of all social groupings and strata concerned.

In its absence, insistence on conformity to the emerging cultural standards of the new national elites is likely to engender increasingly embittered articulations of ethnic consciousness and the expressed need for cultural survival on the part of peripheralised groups. (1991: 63. Emphasis in the original.)

On Afrikaner ethnicity, Willem de Klerk, academic, journalist, and brother to the current South African state president, writes the following in a review of a recent book published by a spokesperson of the Afrikaner nationalist right-wing movement in the country:

The conclusion drawn is that there is no doubt about the existence of an Afrikaner culture; that this culture has the right, the duty and the will to endure in a new South Africa; that Afrikaner culture is rooted in religion, history, ethnicity, and a fatherland; that a unique cultural community exists together with its institutional structures; that Afrikaner nationalism forms a part of this cultural expression; and that 'the freedom of Afrikaner life' must be defended, for otherwise the '*volk*' will become no more than history, one of the numerous colonial relicts left behind in Africa.

I agree with every word. (de Klerk, 1992. My translation.)

De Klerk subsequently pleads for the pursuit of these aims not in the political, but in the communal, Afrikaner cultural, domain.

Both Merle Lipton and Johan Degenaar[12] have articulated views similar to those of Doornbos and de Klerk. They propose a representation of South African society as multi-cultural and democratic, as facilitative of ethnic diversity at the communal level, and prescriptive of constitutionalism at the central level.

To scholars of contemporary South African society, such views pose two scholarly challenges.

In the first place, ethnic communities in South Africa - changing, as they may well be, with their society - need to be researched in relation to other forms of solidarity, not solely as categories of South Africans who are, or are not, being assimilated into South African society.

We have seen that a focus on the macro-level, on South African society as a whole, has been consistently sustained by scholars over the last fifteen years. Such a focus, on its own, leads to questions regarding either nation-building in the society, or regarding partition and secession for different nations within the society. A focus on the communal level, complementary to that on the societal level, is needed.

In the second place, there is a challenge at the level of the society as a whole. It is to identify ways in which the plurality of cultures in South African society may be accommodated without the emergence of ethnic claims either to sovereignty of the central state, or to parts of South African territory.

That there are constraints on the development of democracy that are rooted in racial stratification and consciousness, in class stratification and consciousness, in different forms of state manipulation, and in imperatives simultaneously for growth and redistribution is common cause to scholars of contemporary South African society. The multi-cultural challenge has yet to be addressed seriously. As Degenaar puts it, the task of democracy 'is precisely to depoliticise communal culture in the sense that this culture does not claim sovereignty... but relativises itself on behalf of constitutionalism'[13].

We have considered the three scholarly representations of modern South African society developed over the last fifteen years. We have seen that their relative dominance has shifted during this period. Insofar as the community of scholars picks up the two challenges identified above, a new scholarly representation of modern South Africa may emerge, a representation in which South African identity is defined differently.

Being South African, scholars have claimed, meant being unique, meant being defined within imposed, separate and given compartments. In this sense, there are no South Africans. A new scholarly representation may release South Africans from this stigma by enabling each South African to be both a South African and a member, by choice, of a cultural community. Conceivably, in this sense, there will be South Africans, people who share a common society.

NOTES

1. Horowitz 1991a: 29. See, also, Sharp and McAllister (forthcoming).
2. These citations are given on pp. 63, 26, 93 and 74 respectively.
3. Analyses on which this paragraph is based are found in Chs IV, V, and VI. It is also of interest to note that the continuing debate on the ethnic question within the diminishing ranks of Afrikaner nationalist scholars was largely conducted in Afrikaans, thereby concealing the debate from most other scholars.
4. The recent literature is enormous. See, for example, issues of Indicator South Africa for the years 1990-1992.
5. On the continuing conflict in the country, see, for example, Adam and Moodley 1992, Bekker 1992, Minnaar 1992. On exclusivist Zulu nationalism, see, for example, Adam and Moodley 1992, Maré 1992.
6. On the form of the future South African state, see Friedman and Humphries 1993, Institute of Multi-Party Democracy 1992. On the language question, see Alexander 1990.
7. Douwes Dekker 1991.
8. Hobsbawm 1992: 24,25. My emphasis.
9. Noiriel 1991b.
10. Shaw 1986: 588; Young 1986: 442,454; Vail 1989a: xii.
11. Horowitz 1985: xii
12. Lipton 1985: 12. Degenaar 1993: 23.
13. Degenaar 1993: 23.

BIBLIOGRAPHY

Two separate bibliographies have been developed. The first entitled 'International', refers to works which address the subject matter without a specific focus on South Africa. The second entitled 'South Africa', refers to works in which South African material is central or particularly important. Most, though by no means all, works included in the second list have been written in South Africa, primarily by South African scholars.

International

Alba, R.D. 'Unintended chiaroscuro: the state of knowledge about ethnicity and race in the United States' in Horowitz, D. *op. cit.* 1991b. 35-44.

Amselle J-L and E. M'Bokolo *Au Coeur de l'Ethnie* Paris: Éditions La Découvert 1985.

Amselle, J-L *Logiques métisses: anthropologie de l'identité en Afrique et ailleurs* Paris: Payot 1990.

Anderson, B. *Imagined Communities: Reflections on the origin and spread of nationalism.* London: Verso Editions and New Left Books. 1983.

Avruch, K 'Making Culture, and its costs: review article' *Ethnic and Racial Studies* 15(4) 1992. 614-626.

Blitzer, C 'Preface' in "Research on Ethnicity: a report of a meeting at the Woodrow Wilson International Center for Scholars" 1991

Boucher J, D. Landis, and K.A. Clark (eds) *Ethnic conflict. International perspectives.* London: Sage Publications 1987.

Bratislava Symposium 'Minorities in Politics' International symposium on national minorities in Central Europe. Nov. 13-16 1991

Coulon, C. "Dix ans après: l"Afrique et *Politique africaine*' *Politique Africaine*, 39, 1990, 3-5.

Davis J. *Times and Identity* An Inaugural Lecture delivered before the University of Oxford on 1 May 1991. Oxford: Clarendon Press 1991.

Doornbos, M. "Linking the Future to the Past: Ethnicity and Pluralism' *Review of African Political Economy*, 52, 1991. 53-65.

Epstein, A. *Ethnos and Identity: Three Studies in Ethnicity.* London: Tavistock Publications 1978.

Ghai, D., Y. Ghai, and D. Westendorff 'Ethnicity, development and democracy' in *Peace and Conflict Issues after the Cold War* Geneva: UNESCO 1992 79-103

Gellner, E. *Nations and Nationalism.* Oxford: Basil Blackwell. 1983.

Glazer, N. and D. Moynihan (eds.) *Ethnicity: theory and experience.* Cambridge, Mass., Harvard University Press 1975.

Goldberg, D.T. 'The Semantics of race' *Ethnic and Racial Studies* 15(4) 1992. 543-569.

Harz, Louis *The Founding of New Societies* New York : Harcourt Brace and World 1964.

Hobsbawm, E. 'Nationalism: Whose fault-line is it anyway?' *New Statesman and Society*, 24 April 1992, 23-26.

Horowitz, Donald L *Ethnic groups in Conflict* Berkeley: University of California Press 1985

Horowitz, Donald L "Research on Ethnicity: a report of a meeting at the Woodrow Wilson International Center for Scholars" 1991b.

Klitgaard, R. *Controlling Corruption.* Berkeley: University of California Press 1988.

Klitgaard, R. *Tropical Gangsters: one man's experience with development and decadence in deepest Africa.* London: Tauris 1991.

Martin, D-C 'The Cultural Dimensions of Governance' *Proceedings of the World Bank Annual Conference on Development Economics. 1991* Washington: The World Bank 1992.

Martin, D-C 'The Choices of Identity.' Paper presented at a Conference on Ethnicity, Identity and Nationalism, Rhodes University, Grahamstown, April 1993.

Murphree M. W. 'The salience of ethnicity in African states: a Zimbabwean case study' *Ethnic and Racial Studies* 11(2) 1988. 119-138.

Nash, M. *The Cauldron of Ethnicity in the Modern World* Chicago: University of Chicago Press. 1989

Noiriel, G. *Le creuset français: histoire de l'immigration XIXe-XXe siècle.* Paris: Éditions de Seuil 1988.

Noiriel, G. *La tyrannie du national: le droit d'asile en Europe (1793-1993)* Paris: Calmann-Levy 1991a.

Noiriel, G. 'La question nationale comme objet de l'histoire sociale' *Revue Genèses* 1991b (4) 72-94

Olzak S. and J. Nagel (eds) *Competitive ethnic relations* New York: Academic Press Inc. 1986.

Pieterse, J. N. 'The varieties of ethnic politics and ethnic discourse' Paper (draft) presented at a Conference on Ethnicity, Identity and Nationalism, Rhodes University, Grahamstown, April 1993.

Ranger, T. 'The Invention of Tradition in Colonial Africa', in E.G.Hobsbawm and T. Ranger (eds.), *The Invention of Tradition* Cambridge: Cambridge University Press, 1983.

Roosens E. E. *Creating Ethnicity: the process of ethnogenesis* London: Sage Publications 1989.

Shaw, T.M. 'Ethnicity as the resilient paradigm for Africa: From the 1960s to the 1980s' *Development and Change*, 17, 1986, 587-605.

Southall, A. 'The Ethnic Heart of Anthropology' *Cahiers d'Études africaines*, 100, XXV-4, 1985, 567-572.

Smith, A.D. *The Ethnic Origins of Nations*. Oxford: Basil Blackwell 1986.

Smith, A.D. 'Chosen People: why ethnic groups survive' *Ethnic and Racial Studies* 15(3) 1992. 436-456.

Thompson, Richard H, *Theories of ethnicity: a critical appraisal*. New York: Greenwood Press 1989.

World Bank *The Challenge of Development: world development indicators*. World Bank: Oxford University Press 1991.

Wunsch J. S. and D. Olowu (eds) *The failure of the centralised state: institutions and self-governance in Africa* New York: Westview Press 1990.

Young, M. Crawford 'Nationalism, Ethnicity, and Class in Africa: A Retrospective' *Cahiers d'Études africaines*, 103, XXVI-3, 1986, 421-495.

Yun M. S. 'Ethnonationalism, ethnic nationalism, and mini-nationalism: a comparison of Connor, Smith and Snyder' *Ethnic and Racial Studies* 13(4) 1990 527-541.

South Africa

Adam, H. *Modernising Racial Domination* Berkeley: University of California Press 1971.

Adam, H. 'Towards a democratic transformation' in Schrire, R. (ed.) *op.cit.*1990. 443-458.

Adam, H 'World's Apart: north and south in one state.' *Indicator SA* 10(1) 1992.

Adam, H and H Giliomee *Ethnic Power Mobilized? Can South Africa change?* New Haven: Yale University Press 1979.

Adam, H and K. Moodley *South Africa without Apartheid: dismantling racial domination*. Cape Town: Maskew Miller Longmans 1986

Adam, H and K. Moodley 'The White Mind, Business, and Apartheid' in Keller and Picard, *op.cit.* 1989 139-152.

Adam, H and K. Moodley 'Political Violence. "Tribalism", and Inkatha' *The Journal of Modern African Studies* 30 (3) 1992 484-510.

Alexander, N. *Sow the Wind: contemporary speeches*. Johannesburg: Skotaville Publishers 1985.

Alexander, N. 'The language question' in Schrire, R. (ed.) *Critical Choices for South Africa: an agenda for the 1990s. op.cit.*, 1990 126-146.

Atkinson, D. 'Cities and Citizenship: towards a normative analysis of the urban order in South Africa, with special reference to East London, 1950-1986' unpublished Ph.D (Politics) thesis, University of Natal, Durban, 1991.

Auerbach, F. and D. Welsh 'Education' in van der Horst S. (ed) *op.cit.* 1981 66-89.

Bank, L. 'Angry men and working women: patriarchy, gender relations and economic change in QwaQwa in the 1980s' Paper presented at the Anthropolical Association of Southern Africa Conference, University of the Western Cape, 1989.

Beinart, W. 'Labour migrancy and rural production: Pondoland c. 1900-1950.' in Mayer, P (ed) *op.cit.* 1980. 81-108

Bekker, S. 'The Plural Society and the problem of order' Unpublished Ph.D. thesis, University of Cape Town 1975a

Bekker, S. 'The Pluralist Approach of Pierre van den Berghe' *Social Dynamics*, 1(1) 1975b.

Bekker, S. 'Pluralism and Conflict Regulation' *Philosophical Papers* (Rhodes University, South Africa) Vol VI (2) 1977.

Bekker, S. 'Engaging the state' Inaugural address. Durban: University of Natal 1989

Bekker, S (ed.) *Capturing the Event: Conflict trends in the Natal region 1986-1992*. Durban: Indicator Special Focus, University of Natal 1992.

Bekker S, C. Cross, and N. Bromberger 'Rural poverty in South Africa: A 1992 study using secondary sources' Durban: Centre for Social and Development Studies, University of Natal 1993.

Bekker, S. and C.W.Manona 'Pondoland looking north to Natal: common economic interests or different regional loyalties?' in A. Donaldson et al (eds.) *Undoing Independence: regionalism and the reincorporation of Transkei into South Africa.* Journal of Contemporary African Studies 11(2) 1992. 241-254.

Berger, P and B.Godsell (eds.) *A Future South Africa: Visions, strategies and realities.* Cape Town: Human and Rousseau Tafelberg 1988.

Bindman, G. (ed.) *South Africa: Human Rights and the Rule of Law.* International Commission of Jurists. London: Pinter Publishers. 1988.

Bloom, L. *The Social Psychology of Race Relations.* George Allen and Unwin: London 1971.

Boonzaaier, E. and J.Sharp (eds.) *South African Keywords: the uses and abuses of political concepts.* Cape Town 1988.

Boulle, L. J. *South Africa and the Consociational Option: a constitutional analysis.* Cape Town: Juta and Co. 1984.

Bozzoli, B. (ed.) *Town and Countryside in the Transvaal: Capitalist Penetration and Popular Response.* Johannesburg: Ravan Press 1983.

Bozzoli, B. (ed.) *Class, Community and Conflict: South African perspectives.* Johannesburg: Ravan Press 1987.

Bozzoli, B. 'Les intellectuels et leurs publics face a l'histoire. L'expérience sud-africaine du History Workshop (1878-1988)' L'Histoire face au politique *Politique Africaine* 46 1992. 15-30.

Bradford, H. 'Class contradictions and class alliances: the social nature of ICU leadership 1924-1929' in Lodge, T (ed.) *op. cit.* 1987. 49-73.

Cloete, F., L. Schlemmer and D. van Vuuren (eds.) *Policy Options for a New South Africa.* Pretoria: HSRC Publishers 1991.

Cloete, G. S. 'Etnisiteit en Groepsverteenwoordiging in die Staatskunde - 'n vergelykende studie.' Unpublished Ph.D. thesis, University of Stellenbosch 1981.

Cobbett, W. and R. Cohen (eds.) *Popular Struggles in South Africa.* London: James Currey 1988.

Cobbett, W and B. Nakedi 'The Flight of the Herschelites: ethnic nationalism and land dispossession.' in Cobbett, W. and R. Cohen (eds.) *op.cit.*1988. 77-89.

Coetzee, J.K. (ed.) *Development is for the people.* Johannesburg: Southern Books 1989.

Cohen, R, Y. Muthien and A. Zegeye (eds.) *Repression and Resistance: Insider Accounts of Apartheid.* London: Hans Zell Publishers. 1990.

Comaroff, J. *Body of Power Spirit of Resistance: The culture and history of a South African people.* Chicago: University of Chicago Press 1985.

Copans, J. 'Afrique du Sud: apartheid, culture et politique.' *Cahiers d'Études africaines,* 123, XXXI-3, 1991, 417-423.

Cross C, S Bekker, C Clark and C Wilson. *Searching for Stability: Residential Migration and Community Control in Mariannhill* Rural-Urban Studies Unit, Working Paper No 23. Durban: Centre for Social and Development Studies, 1992. (Cross *et al* (a)).

Cross C, S Bekker, C Clark and R Richards. *Moving On: Migration streams into and out of Inanda.* Durban: Report for the Town and Regional Planning Commission of the Natal Provincial Administration, Pietermaritzburg 1992. (Cross *et al* (b)).

Cross C, S Bekker, and C Clark 'People on the Move: migration streams in the DFR' *Indicator SA,* Vol9/No2, Durban: Centre for Social and Development Studies, University of Natal, 1992 (Cross, C *et al* (c)).

Cross, C. and R. Haines (eds.) *Towards Freehold: Options for land and development in South Africa's Black rural areas.* Cape Town: Juta 1988.

Davenport, R. *South Africa. A Modern History* Johannesburg: Macmillan 1978.

de Beer Z.J. *Multi-Racial South Africa: the reconciliation of forces.* London: Oxford University Press 1961.

de Haas, M and P.Zulu 'Ethnicity and nationalism in post-apartheid South Africa: the case of Natal and the Zulus' Paper presented at the American Anthropological Association's 90th annual meeting. Chicago 1991.

de Klerk, Willem 'Afrikaner kán vir hom 'n toekoms bou.' *Rapport* 1.11.92.

Degenaar, J. 'State and Society: a pluralist approach' *Philosophical Papers* (Rhodes University, South Africa) Vol VI (2) 1977

Degenaar, J. 'The myth of a South African nation' Paper presented at a Conference on Ethnicity, Identity and Nationalism, Rhodes University, Grahamstown, April 1993.

Delius, P. *The land belongs to us.* Johannesburg: Ravan Press 1983.

Douwes Dekker, L. 'Thabong-Welkom: Is this the new South Africa?' Johannesburg: Wits Business School 1991.

Dubow, S. 'Race, civilisation and culture: the elaboration of segregationist discourse in the inter-war years.' in Marks, S and Trapido, S. (eds.) *op.cit.* 1987 71-94

Dubow, S. 'Ethnic Euphemisms and Racial Echoes' Paper presented at a Conference on Ethnicity, Identity and Nationalism, Rhodes University, Grahamstown, April 1993.

du Toit, A. 'Captive to the Nationalist paradigm!. Prof. F.A. van Jaarsveld and the historical evidence for the Afrikaner's ideas on his calling and mission.' *South African Historical Journal.* Vol. 16, 1984.

du Toit, A. 'Puritans in Africa? Afrikaner "Calvinism" and Kuyperian neo-Calvinism in late nineteenth century South Africa.' *Comparative Studies in Society and History.* 27(3) 1985. 209-240.

du Toit, A. and H. Giliomee *Afrikaner Political Thought: analysis and documents. 1 (1780-1850).* Cape Town: David Philip. 1983.

Elphick, R. and H. Giliomee (eds.) *The Shaping of South African society 1652-1840.* Cape Town: Maskew Miller Longman 1989

Frederickson, G. *White supremacy: a comparative study in American and South African history.* New York: Oxford University Press 1981.

Friedman, S. and R. Humphries (eds.) *Federalism and its Foes.* Johannesburg: Centre for Policy Studies 1993.

Gann, L H and P. Duignan *Hope for South Africa?* Stanford, Calif.: Hoover Institution Press 1991.

Gerhart, G. *Black Power in South Africa.* Berkeley: University of California Press 1978.

Giliomee, H. 'Building a new nation: alternative approaches' in Cloete, F *et al.* (eds.) *op.cit.* 1991. 65-86.

Giliomee, H. and L. Schlemmer *Negotiating South Africa's future.* Johannesburg: Southern Books 1989a.

Giliomee, H. and L. Schlemmer *From Apartheid to Nation-building.* Cape Town: Oxford University Press 1989b.

Gordon, R. 'The White Man's Burden.' *Journal of Historical Sociology* 2,1 1989. 41-61.

Greenberg, S. *Race and State in Capitalist Development.* Johannesburg: Ravan Press 1980.

Greenberg, S *Legitimating the Illegitimate: state, markets and resistance in South Africa.* Berkeley: University of California Press 1987.

Grobbelaar, J. 'Ultra-rightwing Afrikaners; a sociological analysis' Unpublished Ph.D. thesis, Sociology, University of South Africa, 1991.

Grobbelaar, J., S. Bekker, and R. Evans *Vir Volk en Vaderland: a guide to the White Right.* Durban: Indicator SA, University of Natal 1989.

Guy, J. *The destruction of the Zulu kingdom.* Johannesburg: Ravan Press 1982.

Guy, J. 'Analysing pre-capitalist societies in Southern Africa' *Journal of Southern African Societies,* 14(1) 1987, 18-37.

Guy, J. 'Debating Ethnicity in South Africa' Paper presented at a conference on Ethnicity, Society and Conflict in Natal, Pietermaritzburg, 1992.

Guy, J. and M. Thabane 'The Ma-Rashea: a participant's perspective' in Bozzoli, B. (ed.) *op.cit.*1987. 436-456

Hackland, B. 'Incorporatist ideology as a response to political struggle: the Progressive Party of South Africa, 1960-1980." Marks, S and Trapido, S. (eds.) *op.cit. 1987* 366-388.

Hanf, T. *et al. South Africa: the prospects of peaceful change.* London: Rex Collings, 1981.

Hanf T. 'The Prospects of Accommodation in Communal Conflicts: a comparative study' in Giliomee, H and Schlemmer, L *Negotiating South Africa's Future* Johannesburg: Southern Books 1989 89-113.

Harries, P. 'Exclusion, Classification and Internal Colonialism: The emergence of ethnicity among the Tsonga-speakers of South Africa' in Vail (ed.), *op. cit.* 1989. 82-117.

Harries, P. 'L'ethnie comme sujet d'histoire en Afrique du Sud', Paper presented at a conference on État, Nation, Ethnicité, Bordeaux, France, November 1992.

Hofmeyr, I. 'Building a nation from words: Afrikaans language, literature and ethnic identity.' Marks, S and Trapido, S. (eds.) *op.cit. 1987* 95-123.

Horowitz, D. L. *A Democratic South Africa ? Constitutional engineering in a divided society* Cape Town: Oxford University Press 1991a.

Human Sciences Research Council (HSRC) *The South African Society: Realities and Future Prospects.* Main Committee: HSRC investigation into intergroup relations. Pretoria 1985.

Human Sciences Research Council (HSRC) *Information Update.* Pretoria 2(4) 1992.

Huntington, S. 'Reform and stability in a modernising multi-ethnic society' Paper delivered at the biennial conference of the South African political science association, Johannesburg: Rand Afrikaanse University 1981.

Indicator South Africa 'New Frontiers: the KwaZulu/Natal debates. Durban: University of Natal. 1987.

Indicator South Africa Fiftieth Edition: South Africa, Present, Past and Future. Durban: University of Natal. 7(4) 1992.

Institute for Multi-Party Democracy. *Towards Democracy* Durban: Journal of the Institute for Multi-Party Democracy, 1992.

James, D. 'A question of ethnicity: Ddzundza Ndebele in a Lebowa village' *Journal of Southern African Studies* 16(1) 1990. 33-54.

Johnson, R.W. *How long will South Africa survive?* London: Macmillan Press 1977.

Johnstone, F.R. *Class, Race and Gold.* London: Routledge and Kegan Paul 1976.

Kane-Berman, J. 'The Apartheid Legacy' in Schrire, R. (ed.) *Critical Choices for South Africa: an agenda for the 1990s. op.cit.*, 1990a 370-392.

Kane-Berman, J. *South Africa's Silent Revolution.* Johannesburg: Southern Books 1990b.

Keller E. and L.Picard (eds.) *South Africa in Southern Africa: domestic change and international conflict.* Boulder, Colorado: Lynne Rienner 1989.

Kiernan, J. Book review of Comaroff 1985 in *Africa* 57(1) 1987: 131-132.

Kinloch, G. *The Sociological Study of South Africa: an introduction.* Johannesburg: Macmillan 1972.

Kotzé, D. J. *Positiewe Nasionalisme.* Cape Town: Tafelberg 1968.

Kuper, L. and M.G.Smith (eds.) *Pluralism in Africa.* California: University of California Press 1969.

Leftwich, A. (ed.) *South Africa: Economic Growth and Political Change.* London 1974.

Legassick, M. 'The National Union of South African students: ethnic cleavage and ethnic segregation in the universities.' *Occasional paper no. 4.* African Studies Centre, University of California, Los Angeles. 1967.

Legum, C. 'Color and Power in the South African situation' *Daedalus, Journal of the American Academy of Arts and Sciences*, Spring 1967, 483-495.

Lipton, M. *Capitalism and Apartheid* Aldershot: Gower 1985.

Lijphart, A 'The Ethnic factor and democratic constitution-making in South Africa' in Keller E and Picard L (eds.) *op.cit.* 1989 13-24

Lodge, T *Black Politics in South Africa.* Johannesburg: Ravan Press 1983.

Lodge, T (ed.) *Resistance and Ideology in Settler Societies.* Johannesburg: Ravan Press 1987.

McAllister, P. 'Work, homestead and the Shades: the ritual interpretation of labour migration among the Gcaleka' in Mayer, P (ed) *op. cit.*1980. 205-254.

Maake N. P. 'Multi-cultural relations in a post-apartheid South Africa' *African Affairs* 91 1992 583-604.

Macmillan, H. 'A Nation Divided? The Swazi in Swaziland and the Transvaal' in Vail (ed.), *op. cit.* 1989. 289-323.

MacMillan, H. 'Economists, apartheid and "the Common Society"' *Social Dynamics* 17(1) 1991 78-100.

Macmillan, H. 'Return to Malungwana Drift - Max Gluckamn, the Zulu Nation and the Common Society.' Paper presented at a conference on Ethnicity, Society and Conflict in Natal, Pietermaritzburg, 1992.

MacNamara, J. 'Brothers and Workmates: Home friend networks in the social life of black migrants in a gold mine hostel.' in Mayer, P (ed) *op. cit.*1980. 305-340.

Manganyi, C. and A. du Toit (eds.) *Political violence and the struggle in South Africa.* London: Macmillan 1990

Maré, G. *Brothers Born of Warrior Blood: Politics and Ethnicity in South Africa.* Johannesburg: Ravan Press 1992.

Maré, G and G. Hamilton *An Appetite for Power.* Johannesburg: Ravan Press 1987.

Marks, S. *The Ambiguities of Dependence in South Africa.* Johannesburg: Ravan Press 1986.

Marks, S. 'Patriotism, Patriarchy and Purity: Natal and the Politics of Zulu Ethnic Consciousness' in Vail (ed.), *op. cit.* 1989. 215-240.

Marks, S and N. Andersson 'The Epidemiology and Culture of Violence' in Manganyi, C. and A. du Toit *op.cit.* 1990. 29-69

Marks, S and S. Trapido (eds.) *The Politics of Race, Class and Nationalism in Twentieth Century South Africa.* London: Longman 1987.

Marquard, L. *A Federation of Southern Africa.* London: Oxford University Press 1971.

Mathews A.S. 'Security, freedom and reform' in Schrire, R. (ed.) *Critical Choices for South Africa: an agenda for the 1990s.* Cape Town: Oxford University Press 1990.

Matthews, J. 'Inside Story' in *Towards Democracy* Durban: Journal of the Institute for Multi-Party Democracy, 1992.

Mayer, P. 'Class, status, and ethnicity as perceived by Johannesburg Africans' in Thompson, L and J Butler (eds.) *Change in Contemporary South Africa. op.cit.* 1975.

Mayer, P. (ed) *Black Villagers in an Industrial Society*. Cape Town: Oxford University Press 1980.

Mayer, P. and I. Mayer *Townsmen or Tribesmen*. Cape Town: Oxford University Press 1974.

Meillassoux C.(ed.) *Verrouillage ethnique en Afrique du Sud*. Paris: OUA 1988.

Meillassoux, C and C. Messiant (eds.) *Génie social et manipulations culturelles en Afrique du Sud*. Paris: Arcantère éditions 1991.

Mphahlele, E. *Down Second Avenue* London 1959.

Minnaar, A. (ed.) *Patterns of Violence: case studies of conflict in Natal*. Pretoria: Human Sciences Research Council 1992.

Moodie T. D. *The Rise of Afrikanerdom* Berkeley: University of California Press 1974.

Motlhabi, M. *Toward a new South Africa: Issues and objects in the ANC/Government negotiation for a non-racial democratic society*. Johannesburg: Skotaville Publishers 1992.

Muller, C.F.J. (ed.) *500 Years: A History of South Africa*. Pretoria: Academica 1969

Ngubane, J.K. *Conflict of Minds: changing power dispositions in South Africa*. New York: Books in focus 1979.

Nolutshungu, S. *Changing South Africa*. Manchester: Manchester University Press 1982.

Peires, J. *The House of Phalo*. Johannesburg: Ravan Press 1981.

Posel, D. 'Rethinking the "race-class debate" in South African historiography' *Social Dynamics* 9(1) 1983, 50-66.

Posel, D. 'The language of domination, 1978-1983' in Marks, S and Trapido, S. (eds.) *The Politics of Race, Class and Nationalism in Twentieth Century South Africa.*, op.cit. 1987 419-444

Ramphele, Mamphela. See Wilson and Ramphele.

Rex, J. 'The Plural Society: the South African case.' *Race*, 12(4) 1971 401-313.

Rhoodie, N. J. *Die moderne etniese problematiek*. Geleentheidspublikasie nr. 24 Pretoria: HSRC 1985.

Rhoodie, N. J. and M. P. Couper *'n Vergelykende ontleding van drie Afrikaner-dominante gemeenskappe se persepsies van Wit-Swart-verhoudinge in Suid-Afrika*. Geleentheidspublikasie nr. 33 Pretoria: HSRC 1986.

Rothchild, D. 'From exhortation to incentive strategies: mediation efforts in South Africa in the mid-1980s' in Keller, E & Picard L. (eds) *op.cit.*, 1989 25-48.

Saul, J. 'Class, race and the future of socialism' in Cobbett, W. and R. Cohen (eds.) *op.cit* 1988. 210-228.

Savage, M. 'Major Patterns of Group Interaction in South African Society' in Thompson L and J Butler (eds) *Change in Contemporary South Africa. op.cit.* 1975. 280-302.

Schlemmer, L. 'Theories of the Pural Society and Change in South Africa' *Social Dynamics* 3(1) 1977. 3-16.

Schlemmer, L. 'Dimensions of Turmoil: position paper on current violence in South Africa' *Policy Issues and Actors* 4 (2). Pretoria: HSRC 1991

Schlemmer, L. 'South Africa in the shadow of the past' Indicator SA 9(4), 7-14 Durban: University of Natal 1992.

Schlemmer, L, V. Moller and P. Stopforth 'Black Communities, Socio-Political Reform, and the Future' CASS 11/80. Centre for Applied Social Sciences, University of Natal, Durban 1980.

Schrire, R. (ed.) *Critical Choices for South Africa: an agenda for the 1990s*. Cape Town: Oxford University Press 1990.

Schutte, G. 'Netherlands, cradle of apartheid?' *Ethnic and Racial Studies* 10(4) 1987, 392-414.

Shanafelt, R. 'Worker solidarity, differentiation, and the manipulation of ethnicity: conflict at the Vaal Reefs, 1984-1986.' in Davis, R.H. (ed.) *Apartheid Unravels*. Florida: University of Florida Press 1991. 119-140.

Sharp, J. 'Can we study ethnicity? A critique of fields of study in South African anthropology' *Social Dynamics* 6 (1) 1980 1-16.

Sharp, J. and E. Boonzaaier 'Ethnic Identity as Performance: Lessons from Namaqualand' Paper presented at a Conference on Ethnicity, Identity and Nationalism, Rhodes University, Grahamstown, April 1993.

Sharp. J and P. McAllister 'Ethnicity, Identity and Nationalism: insights and the South African debate' *Anthropology Today* (forthcoming)

Shillington, K. *The colonisation of the Southern Tswana 1870-1900*. Johannesburg: Ravan Press 1985

Simkins, C. *The Prisoners of Tradition and the Politics of Nation Building*. Johannesburg: SAIRR 1988.

Simson, H. *The social origins of Afrikaner fascism and its apartheid policy*. Uppsala Sudies in Economic History, 21. Stockholm: Almquist and Wikell 1980.

Slabbert, Van Zyl 'Ideological change, Afrikaner nationalism, and pragmatic racial domination in South Africa' in Thompson, L and J Butler (eds.) *Change in Contemporary South Africa, op.cit.*, 1975.

Slabbert, Van Zyl 'Reform and Revolt: 1983 to 1988' in Giliomee, H. and L. Schlemmer *op. cit*1989a. 75-82

Slabbert, Van Zyl 'Book review of Horowitz, D L "A Democratic South Africa ? Constitutional engineering in a divided society"' *African Studie*s 49(2) 1990 112-116.

Slabbert, Van Zyl and D. Welsh *South Africa's Options: Strategies for sharing power.* Cape Town: David Philip 1979.

Spiegel, A. 'Rural differentiation and the diffusion of migrants labour remittances in Lesotho' in Mayer, P (ed) *op. cit* 1980. 109-169

Study Project on Christianity in Apartheid Society (Sprocas) *South Africa's Political Alternatives.* No.10. Johannesburg: Ravan Press 1973.

Stadler, A. *The Political Economy of Modern South Africa.* Johannesburg: David Philip 1987.

Stone, J. 'Book review of Horowitz (1991a)' *Ethnic and Racial Studies* 15(4) 1992 634-636.

Surplus People's Project (*S.P.P.*) *General Overview: Vol. 1. Forced Removals in South Africa.* Cape Town: S.P.P. 1983.

Suttner, R. 'African customary Law - Its social and ideological function in South Africa.' in Lodge, T (ed.) *op. cit.* 1987. 119-143.

Thompson, L. *The Political Mythology of Apartheid.* New Haven: Yale University Press 1985.

Thompson, L. and J. Butler (eds.) *Change in Contemporary South Africa.* Berkeley: University of California Press. 1975.

Urban Foundation *Policies for a New Urban Future nos.1-10* Johannesburg: The Urban Foundation 1989, 1990.

Vail, L (ed.) *The Creation of Tribalism in Southern Africa* Claremont: David Philip 1989a.

Vail, L. 'Introduction: Ethnicity in Southern African History' in Vail (ed). 1-19, 1989b.

van den Berghe, P. *Caneville.* Middletown, Conn.: Wesleyan University Press, 1964.

van den Berghe, P. *South Africa: a study in Conflict.* Berkeley: University of Berkeley Press, 1967.

van den Berghe, P. 'South Africa after thirty years' *Social Dynamics* 16(2) 1990 16-37.

van der Horst, S. (ed.) *Race discrimination in South Africa: a review.* Cape Town: David Philip 1981.

van der Merwe, S. 'The government's framework for constitutional change and negotiation' in Giliomee, H. and L. Schlemmer *Negotiating South Africa's future. op.cit.* 1989.

van Rooyen, J. 'An Assessment of the White Rightwing in South African Politics with reference to its origins, strength, socio-economic and psychological matrixes, and its political options and strategies: 1969-1991' Unpublished Ph.D. thesis, Political Studies, University of Cape Town 1991.

West, M. *Bishops and Prophets in a Black City.* Cape Town: David Philip 1975.

Wiechers, M. 'The law and ethnicity' Unpublished paper presented at a conference on Identity and Ethnicity. CEAN, Bordeaux, France 1992.

Wilson, F. 'The political implications for blacks of economic changes now taking place in South Africa' in Thompson, L and J Butler (eds.) *Change in Contemporary South Africa. op.eit.* 1975.

Wilson, F. and M. Ramphele *Uprooting poverty: the South African challenge.* Cape Town: David Philip 1989.

Wilson, M. and L. Thompson (eds.) *A History of South Africa to 1870.* Cape Town: David Phillip 1986.

Wolpe, H. *Race, class and the apartheid state.* Paris: UNESCO Press 1988.

Wright H. M. *The burden of the present: liberal-radical controversy over South African history* Cape Town: David Philip 1977.

Wright, J. 'Politics, ideology and the Invention of 'Nguni'' in Lodge, T (ed.) *op. cit.*1987. 96-118.

Wright, J. 'Political Mythology and the Making of Natal's Mfecane' *Canadian Journal of African Studies* 23(2) 1989. 272-291.

Wright, J. 'Notes on the Politics of being "Zulu". 1820-1920.' Paper presented at a conference on Ethnicity, Society and Conflict in Natal, Pietermaritzburg, 1992.

Zulu, P. 'Resistance in the townships - an overview' in Fatima Meer (ed.) *Resistance in the townships.* Durban: Madiba 1989.

Zulu P. 'The Melting Pot: bridging divided societies' in *Indicator South Africa* Fiftieth Edition, *op.cit.* 1992.

Index